# McNamara's Folly

## *The Use of Low-IQ Troops in the Vietnam War*

*plus*
*The Induction of*
*Unfit Men, Criminals, and Misfits*

## Hamilton Gregory

INFINITY PUBLISHING

Copyright © 2015 by Hamilton Gregory

ISBN 978-1-4958-0548-6
ISBN 978-1-4958-0549-3 eBook


Published June 2015

Cover: The photo is of a model for the stock photo agency Shutterstock. Copyright by John Gomez.

INFINITY PUBLISHING
1094 New DeHaven Street, Suite 100
West Conshohocken, PA 19428-2713
Toll-free (877) BUY BOOK
Local Phone (610) 941-9999
Fax (610) 941-9959
Info@buybooksontheweb.com
www.buybooksontheweb.com

Dedicated to the memory of
Merrell,
my beloved wife and best friend

# Contents

# Illustrations

# Author's Notes

1. I am aware that words like *moron, retarded, fatso,* and *dwarf* are considered insensitive and offensive in society today, but I use them because they were widely used in the 1960s, and it would mar the historical accuracy of my report if I replaced them with words that are kinder. Likewise, I sometimes quote individuals whose descriptions are harsh and unsympathetic, but I have included them to document how men who were "different" were viewed and treated in those days.

2. The names and certain other identifying features of the men at Fort Benning have been changed to protect the privacy of the individuals and their families.

# Prologue

In 1966, the U.S. war in Vietnam was heating up rapidly, and President Lyndon Johnson and his Secretary of Defense, Robert McNamara, were faced with a problem: The Armed Forces needed more and more troops for the war zone, but there was a shortage of men who were considered fair game for the military draft. There were plenty of men of draft age (18-26) in America, but most of them were unavailable. Many were attending college, using student deferments to avoid the draft. Others had found safe havens in the National Guard and Reserves, which by and large were not sent to Vietnam. Still others were disqualified because they scored poorly on the military's mental and physical entrance tests.

How could Johnson and McNamara round up enough men to send to war? They realized that they would anger the vote-powerful middle class if they drafted college boys and if they sent National Guardsmen and Reservists to Vietnam. So instead they decided to induct the low-scoring men, whom Johnson referred to (in a secret White House tape) as "second-class fellows." On October 1, 1966, McNamara launched a program called Project 100,000, which lowered mental standards. Men who had been unqualified for military duty the day before were now deemed qualified. By the end of the war, McNamara's program had taken 354,000 substandard men into the Army, Marine Corps, Air Force, and Navy. Among the troops, these men were often known as "McNamara's Morons" or "the Moron Corps" or "McNamara's Boys."

Military leaders—from William Westmoreland, the commanding general in Vietnam, to lieutenants and sergeants at the platoon level—viewed McNamara's program as a disaster. Because many of the Project 100,000 men were slow learners, they had difficulty absorbing necessary training. Because many of them were incompetent in combat, they endangered not only themselves but their comrades as well.

A total of 5,478 low-IQ men died while in the service, most of them in combat. Their fatality rate was three times as high as that of other GIs. An estimated 20,270 were wounded, and some were permanently disabled (including an estimated 500 amputees).

There were also tens of thousands of other "second-class" men who were not part of Project 100,000 but were inducted despite medical defects (such as missing fingers and blindness in one eye), psychiatric disorders, social maladjustment, and criminal backgrounds. Military leaders didn't want them, but were forced to accept them. We don't know how many of them died or were wounded.

While I was in the Army (1967-1970), I got to know some of McNamara's substandard soldiers, and I vowed that someday I would tell their stories and give the historical background. This book is the fulfillment of that vow.

# Part One

# *Bravo Company*

# 1
# Mesmerized by Dog Tags

One morning in the summer of 1967, I was seated with over 100 men in a room at the Armed Forces induction center in Nashville, Tennessee. It was the height of the Vietnam War, and I had volunteered for service in the U.S. Army.

A sergeant walked into the room and announced that all of us would leave soon to travel to Fort Benning, Georgia, to begin our Army training. Then he asked, "Is anyone here a college graduate?"

I raised my hand, and he motioned me to follow him. He took me down a hallway to a bench where a young man was sitting. He informed me that the man was named Johnny Gupton, who was also being assigned to Fort Benning. "I want you to take charge of Gupton," he said. "Go with him every step of the way." Without bothering to lower his voice, he explained that Gupton could neither read nor write and would need help in filling out paperwork when we arrived at Benning. Then he added, "Make sure he doesn't get lost. He's one of McNamara's Morons."

I had never heard the term, and I was surprised that the sergeant would openly insult Gupton. In a few weeks I would learn that McNamara's Morons was a term that many officers and NCOs (non-commissioned officers) used to refer to low-IQ men who were taken into the military under a program devised by Defense Secretary Robert S. McNamara to raise their IQs and mold them into productive soldiers. (I will give historical details in Part Three of this book.)

The sergeant left us for a while. When he returned, he gave me a sealed envelope that contained my personnel records and Gupton's. I was instructed to give the package to the sergeants when I arrived at Fort Benning.

Gupton and I and the other men who were assigned to Fort Benning rode on buses to the airport, where we boarded an airplane for a flight to Georgia. We were headed toward Basic Combat Training, a rigorous, eight-week training regimen that every person who entered the Army had to go through. Its goal was to transform civilians into soldiers who were strong and agile, able to use rifles and grenades in combat, and thoroughly adapted to the Army culture of unquestioning obedience to commands from superiors.

I was nervous about the rigors ahead, but I felt brave and stoic and important. I envisioned losing weight and bulking up my muscles, becoming "a lean green fighting machine," as the popular saying had it. I looked beyond the eight weeks of hell and pictured myself going home on leave looking hard and fit.

I tried to make small talk with Gupton, but he didn't say much. I asked him what state he was from, but he didn't know. (I later found out that he was from Tennessee. He lived in one of the isolated "poverty pockets" in the Appalachian Mountains in the eastern part of the state.) He spoke with a hillbilly accent and used mountain phrases like "I knowed it," and "sody water" (for soda pop). He looked unhealthily thin.

I was surprised that he knew nothing about the situation he was in. He didn't understand what basic training was all about, and he didn't know that America was in a war. I tried to explain what was happening, but at the end, I could tell that he was still in a fog.

We traveled to Atlanta and then to Columbus, Georgia, where we transferred to Army buses, along with other new trainees, for the trip to Fort Benning. It was late at night when we arrived at the Reception Station, where we would spend a week before the official start of basic training. As we stepped off our bus, we were screamed at by loud, menacing sergeants, who accused us of being "girls" and "pussies" and "civilian scum." We were ordered to stand in a line, and I made sure that Gupton stood next to me.

Most of us arrived carrying a gym bag or a sack filled with our personal possessions. A sergeant led us in front of a large barrel and ordered us to surrender all knives, pistols, bullets, brass knuckles, drugs, alcoholic beverages, subversive literature, and pornographic materials. We were told we would not be punished if we complied now, but if we were discovered to have forbidden items later, we would be sent to the stockade, and the time spent imprisoned would not count as part of our two- or three-year obligation.

Neither Gupton nor I possessed any undesirable items, but roughly a third of the men turned in contraband: pistols, knives, sex magazines, booze, and marijuana. Everyone laughed as each man walked up to the barrel, pulled out his forbidden possession, and grudgingly put it in. One man asked if he could get his knife back someday. No, the sergeant said, the weapons would be sold, the drugs would be destroyed, and the magazines would be placed in Army hospitals for sick and wounded GIs. But if GIs in hospitals could have sex magazines, why couldn't we? We would be isolated for two months, the sergeant explained, and it would do us no good to think about sex. When we got out of basic training, we would be allowed to have *Playboy* or any other magazine.

Then we joined hundreds of other new arrivals in an auditorium that resembled a high school gym. We sat on bleachers and listened to sergeants give us an orientation. One sergeant told us, with sarcasm in his voice, that our mommies and daddies and girlfriends might be worried sick over whether we had made it to Fort Benning. To prevent a massive wave of frantic phone calls, each of us was given a "safe arrival card," a pre-stamped postcard to reassure our loved ones that we had reached our destination. On one side, we were supposed to put the name and address of next of kin. On the other side was a printed message, with a couple of blanks that we needed to fill in. The message began as follows:

Dear _____,
This is to inform you that _____ has arrived safely at the Reception Station at Fort Benning, Georgia, where he will remain until assigned to a basic training company.

We were told that this was an official U.S. Army postcard, so we should refrain from writing anything raunchy. The sergeant said, "Don't be like the trainee who went through here and wrote 'Dear Darlene. This is to inform you that Sugar Dick has arrived safely...'"

There was a roar of laughter—but nothing from Gupton. I glanced at him and saw that he apparently failed to "get it." This was the first indication I had that he was utterly unable to understand and appreciate humor.

Because he could not read or write, I filled out his card for him. Unfortunately, he did not know his home address. As for the name of a parent or loved one, the only thing I could elicit was "Granny"—he was unable to give me her full name. On the card, I wrote a note asking that someone please look at Gupton's personnel file to get his home address.

The next morning, we were given our dress uniform and shoes, two sets of fatigues, a cap, a belt, two pairs of combat boots, underwear, and socks—plus a duffel bag to keep everything in.

A clerk gave each of us a box, which we were ordered to fill with our civilian clothes and the bag or sack that we brought from home. We were told that we would not need them anymore, and besides, the Army wanted to discourage us from using them to go AWOL (absent without leave)—the Army's term for running away. Once packed, each box was sealed, and we had to write our name and home address. I advised Gupton to send nothing home. In the first place, he did not know his address, but even more importantly, his stuff was worthless—just shabby, smelly clothes and a pair of worn-out loafers. "Throw it all in the trash," I advised.

We were photographed and fingerprinted, and made to stand in line for immunizations for cholera, smallpox, plague, yellow fever, tetanus, and typhoid. The immunizations were delivered by a medic using an air gun. We had to present our upper right arm, and the medic would hold the gun against the skin and quickly fire a shot of fluid through the skin. Although no needles were used, many of the men—including Gupton—were freaked out. I had to coax Gupton and hold his left arm to steady his trembling body during the process.

We were taken to a barber to get our heads shaved. As each man sat in the chair, the others laughed at him and made jokes. The barber gave me about 10 quick, hard strokes with his clippers, as if I were a sheep being sheared. "Ninety cents!" he shouted. "Next man in the chair!" I looked in the mirror and saw a new and uglier self. My face had always been goofy-looking, but now I looked positively moronic.

Gupton's new combat boots provided a challenge. He could tie the laces, but the knot was primitive and ineffective. I tried to teach him how to make a standard knot, to no avail. So I ended up tying his boots every morning. Fortunately, shoe shining was a different story. After I showed him the proper way to spit-shine his boots, he would apply polish and buff them every night with much success. His boots were always resplendent, and he seemed to take great pride in them.

We were each issued two identical dog tags, stainless-steel rectangles worn on a chain around the neck, to identify us in case we were injured or killed. We were required to wear them at all times, even while showering or sleeping. Engraved on the tags were name, service number, blood type, and religious denomination. If you were wounded in combat, the blood type (for example "O POS" for "O Positive") enabled medics to quickly give you the right kind of blood. If you were dying, the denominational preference let the Army know which kind of cleric (such as priest or rabbi) to summon to administer last rites. If you died, one of the two tags was kept on the body, while the other was retained for official records (and ultimately given to a family member).

In 1967, the service number was 8 digits preceded by a prefix such as RA (Regular Army) for men who had volunteered and had to serve three years, US (United States Selective Service) for men who were drafted and had to serve only two years, and NG (National Guard). I was RA, Gupton was US. (During the next two years, the Army transitioned from service numbers to Social Security numbers for identification.) We were supposed to memorize our service number and say it quickly if a sergeant or officer demanded it. I worked with Gupton to help him memorize his number. After intensive drilling, he could say it, but the next day, he would have forgotten it.

He was mesmerized by his dog tags. He would stare at them, fondle them, and from time to time he would have me read aloud and explain the wording. I always went along with his requests. In a letter to my fiancée, I wrote, "These little pieces of metal provide him with endless fascination."

# 2

# A Thief in the Barracks

After a week at the Reception Station, we were ready to move to basic training, and we were taken to a nearby field. We were told that we would soon constitute Bravo Company, and our commanding officer, Captain Bosch, introduced himself. He looked rugged and stern. He was an airborne ranger who had recently returned from combat in Vietnam. He told us he had been looking over incoming trainees, and he chose us for Bravo Company because we looked like a tough bunch. He said he was going to train us to win every trophy that Fort Benning offered. In fact, we would become one of the best basic training companies in the entire U.S. Army. Most important of all, we would be going to Vietnam, and he wanted us to be in top shape, so that we could kill Charlie and win the war. (Charlie was the nickname for our enemy in Vietnam, the Viet Cong, and was derived from the fact that they were called VC for short. In radio transmissions, the military used certain words to stand for letters of the alphabet. For example, a radio operator would say "Delta Company" instead of "D Company," to ensure accuracy. In the case of VC, the radio operator would say Victor Charlie, which got shortened by the troops to simply Charlie.)

After he finished his remarks, Captain Bosch allowed us to ask questions about what to expect. Yes, we would have to crawl under live machine-gun fire. No, we would not be permitted to go home on leave until basic training was over. No, goddammit, it was not true that we would be served powdered eggs for breakfast. Someone was telling us fairy tales. We would never,

ever be served powdered eggs in basic. American GIs were the best-fed, best-equipped soldiers in the world. Charlie, on the other hand, got only a sack of rice, a few scraps of chicken, and a fermented fish sauce called *nuoc mam*—and sometimes Charlie didn't even get that.

The men of Bravo Company were ordered to collect our duffel bags and move out. But something was wrong: eight names, including mine and Gupton's, were not on the roster. The first sergeant called the eight of us together and told us that our orders had been misplaced. So the rest of the company went on without us, while we waited for orders. When night came, there were still no orders, so the first sergeant introduced us to a Sergeant Slater, who said he would let us spend the night in his barracks. He made us take off our boots before we entered. "These floors are sparkling and I don't want you to mess them up," he said. "And I don't want you using my wall lockers, do you understand? You'd just stink 'em up."

We took off our boots before entering, and when we undressed, we put our clothes on the floor instead of in the wall lockers.

The next morning we discovered that someone had stolen the cash out of our wallets. We estimated that about $200 was taken. (This amount would be worth $1,400 in today's money.) Earlier in the week, we had been given $50 advance pay so that we could go to the PX (Post Exchange), a department store for military personnel, and buy necessities, such as shoe polish, Brasso (metal polish), razor blades, shaving cream, and toothpaste. Our wallets had contained the money left over from our PX visit, plus whatever cash we had brought from home.

We tried unsuccessfully to find Sergeant Slater, then we went to see the first sergeant in the orderly room. He took down our names and the amounts stolen, and said he would report the matter to the MPs (military police).

"Could I call them myself?" I asked.

He looked startled, and said, "No, we'll take this through the chain of command. The MPs will come around to your new unit in a day or so to talk to you."

"You know," I said, "it's a shame that Sergeant Slater told us not to use the wall lockers. If we had used them, we could have heard someone opening the metal doors."

"He told you not to use the wall lockers, huh?" he said. I think he was trying to sound surprised, but the sheepish look on his face convinced me that he was collaborating with Slater. After all, it was the first sergeant who couldn't find our orders the day before.

I realized that we eight had been singled out because all of us (including me with my goofy face) looked like dummies who were unlikely to go to the MPs or write letters to members of Congress. Once we were transferred to our basic training company, we would have no time or energy to pursue the matter. The first sergeant and Sergeant Slater had developed an effective form of thievery that they probably repeated frequently.

Fortunately, my wallet had a secret compartment, which contained a few $20 bills. Gupton was completely wiped out, so I gave him $20. Although I had outfoxed the thief by having a hidden stash, my pride was wounded. How could I have been so stupid as to leave my wallet on the floor? I could have tucked it in my underwear.

By late morning our orders magically materialized, and we were transported to Bravo Company. I knew that the MPs would never come around to interview us, and I was right.

# 3

# An Old Black Shoelace

Bravo Company was made up of four platoons, with 45-50 trainees apiece. Each platoon had its own two-story wooden barracks, and each floor had an open bay filled with rows of double-decker bunks. I bunked with Gupton, giving him the bottom bunk, while I took the top. Each of us was assigned a wall locker and a foot locker to store our gear and personal possessions.

Captain Bosch was assisted by two lieutenants and 13 NCOs. Our platoon's primary NCO was Drill Sergeant Boone, who had recently spent a year in combat in Vietnam.

We were issued M-14 rifles, but no ammunition—yet—and we focused on what the Army called "close-order drill," including how to maneuver and march in step with the rest of the platoon and how to handle and carry our rifles correctly. At first, Gupton had trouble distinguishing left and right, which prevented him from marching in step ("left, right, left, right") and knowing which way to turn for commands like "left face!" and "right flank, march!" So Sergeant Boone tied an old black shoelace around Gupton's right wrist to help him remember which side of his body was the right side, and he placed a rubber band on the left wrist to denote the left side of the body. The shoelace and rubber band helped, but Gupton was a bit slow in responding. For example, he learned how to execute "left face" and "right face," but he was a fraction of a second behind everyone else.

One of my platoon mates, Flewellen, an easygoing guy who became my best friend in basic, took an interest in Gupton and helped me prepare him for inspections. He also took it upon himself to teach Gupton how to tie his bootlaces correctly. He patiently worked with him in the evenings until Gupton mastered the skill. Gupton was proud of himself as he demonstrated his new skill.

Drill sergeants were not allowed to hit trainees, but they could punish by assigning push-ups, the number depending upon the whim of the sergeant. The most repetitions required were 50—for dropping your rifle. "Go on down with it!" Sergeant Boone would snap, as soon as he heard a rifle hit the ground. A trainee had to have the rifle resting on the back of his hands while he did the push-ups.

Every man was ordered to do push-ups at least once during the day, whether he erred or not. "Do you like Georgia?" Sergeant Boone asked one man. The trainee said no. "Well, then, get down and start pushing it away," the sergeant growled.

We had to run everywhere we went, even when not in formation. If a sergeant saw a man walking, he would shout, "Drop!" which meant the trainee must go down into the push-up position. Then he performed the number of push-ups dictated by the sergeant. Before he was allowed to get up, he had to shout, "Permission to recover, Drill Sergeant." If the sergeant said, "Re-cover!" the trainee could jump up and run on his way. If the sergeant said nothing, the trainee had to stay in what the sergeants called the "front leaning rest position" (the "up" stage of push-ups) until he was permitted to get up. This position was painful if kept for more than a minute. One of the sergeants loved to torment Gupton by assigning a certain number of push-ups and then hiding. When Gupton became weary of the agonizing wait and tried to sneak away, the sergeant would jump out, scream at him, and order more push-ups.

Though he couldn't hit us, Sergeant Boone could do violence to our possessions. With righteous indignation, he would stomp on boots poorly shined. If he didn't like the way a bunk was made, he would tear off the blanket and the sheets and dump the mattress on the floor. Then he would give the owner of the bunk a few minutes to make it right, all the while standing over him and screaming in his ear.

Gupton was unable to make his bunk to strict Army specifications, so Flewellen and I would do the job for him every morning, thus sparing him from suffering wrath for a less-than-perfect bunk. Because he was able to polish his boots to a high sheen, he was never punished for unshined boots. But he was constantly harassed (and dropped for push-ups) for failure to use correct "military courtesy." We were taught to salute and say "Sir" when interacting with an officer, but we were forbidden to extend the same courtesies to sergeants. The drill sergeants would sternly correct a trainee if he said "Sir" to a sergeant while an officer was present. When an officer was not around, however, they tried to salvage some of their pride by saying, "Don't call me 'Sir'! I *work* for a living." (Incidentally, the Army way differed from the Marine Corps tradition—as shown in popular war movies—of sergeants being addressed as "sir.")

Gupton had difficulty in distinguishing between officers and sergeants. Flewellen and I tried to show him that lieutenants and captains had bars on their collars, while sergeants had stripes on their sleeves, but he would get confused and say "Sir" to sergeants and "Sergeant" to officers, and he would sometimes salute sergeants.

We did a lot of physical training, such as sit-ups, pull-ups, push-ups, and low crawls, and Captain Bosch led us on cross-country runs. I performed poorly because I was unathletic and out of shape. What made matters worse was exercising in the middle of the day when the heat and humidity were oppressive and debilitating.

While running, we would sing songs like:

*I wanna go to Viet Nam!*
*I wanna kill some Viet Cong!*

The songs helped distract my mind from my physical misery.

Our platoon was involved in constant competition with the company's three other platoons. Which platoon could run the fastest mile? Which could have the cleanest barracks? If we did well in PT (physical training) and inspections, we were praised and given prizes such as free time on a Saturday afternoon, but if we did poorly we were punished (extra push-ups, extra runs) and denied privileges such as weekend time to use pay phone booths to call home.

# 4

# "Weaklings and Fatties and Dummies"

One morning, as the 185 trainees of Bravo Company were assembled in front of Captain Bosch, he called out the names of about 15 men, including me and Gupton. We were ordered to come forth and stand in a line in front of the Captain. He announced that we had been identified as being deficient. "You're the scum of this company—a goddamn bunch of weaklings and fatties and dummies," he said. From now on, we would be known as the Muck Squad. "You know what muck is? That's the shit at the bottom of a sewage pit. That's what you are—worthless shit. I'm gonna run your asses all day long." He said that Bravo Company had a good chance of compiling the highest average on the final PT test of any company at Fort Benning, but that we threatened to drag down the company average.

We were still members of our original platoons, but whenever Captain Bosch called for the Muck Squad, we had to leave our comrades and line up in front of him. We received physical training beyond what we received with our platoons. It was often given before lunch and after dinner.

Someone in the barracks discovered that Gupton thought a nickel was more valuable than a dime because it was bigger in size. I saw him being cheated by a trainee who said, "I'll give you this big nickel if you'll give me your little dime." Today this deception may seem inconsequential because a nickel and a dime are no longer worth much, but in 1967 a nickel would buy a Hershey's candy bar, and a dime would buy a 6-ounce glass bottle of Coca-Cola. After I witnessed the trickery, I took all of his money from him and told him to see me if he wanted to buy anything. Word of Gupton's ignorance about coins apparently spread to the officers because one day, as the Muck Squad lined up, Captain Bosch appeared with several visiting officers, and the first thing they did was show Gupton a nickel and a dime and ask him which one he would prefer. They all grinned when he pointed at the nickel.

Then the visitors stood in front of one man at a time and asked questions, such as "Who's the President of the United States?" This question was one that most of the men could not answer. One of the officers looked at me, probably noting my goofy face, and asked, "Where are we fighting a war?"

"Vietnam, Sir."

"Where is Vietnam located?"

I replied with as much erudition as I could muster. "Sir, Vietnam is situated in Asia, directly south of China and adjacent to Laos and Cambodia."

He looked surprised at my intelligent response, and his fellow officers grinned. "He's a college graduate," interjected Captain Bosch, "but he's badly out of shape."

One of the visitors, who was a captain, asked Gupton, "Which rank is higher—a captain or a general?"

Gupton was speechless for a few moments and then stammered, "I don't know, Drill Sergeant."

"*Drill Sergeant?*" the officer yelled. He pointed to his insignia and said, "Don't you know these two bars mean captain? Don't you know you're supposed to say sir?"

Captain Bosch said, "Can you believe this idiot was drafted? I tell you who else is an idiot. Fuckin' Robert McNamara. How can he expect us to win a war if we draft these morons?"

Captain Bosch's contemptuous remark about Defense Secretary McNamara was typical of the comments I often heard from career Army men, who detested McNamara's lowering of enlistment standards in order to bring low-IQ men into the ranks.


In the early days of basic, the physical challenges were difficult, but even worse was the psychological coercion. A superior was in your face constantly, yelling at you and accusing you of screwing up. All of this was hard on everyone, and it was especially hard on Gupton, who seemed unnerved and frightened by the noise and anger.

He was bewildered by the sergeants' slang. "Take off them Air Force gloves!" meant we should take our hands out of our pockets. Gupton took the term literally and didn't understand why he was being accused of wearing gloves. If a sergeant ordered, "Kill them snakes!" he meant that we must tuck the bow-knot of our boot laces inside the tops of our boots. Snakes? Gupton was baffled—he didn't see any snakes.

We heard rumors that Captain Bosch had lost many of his men in combat in Vietnam. If true, this could explain his emphasis on intense training. He often quoted the Army slogan, "More sweat in training, less blood in combat." And he sometimes made references to Vietnam. One day he was supervising the Muck Squad as we tried to negotiate the horizontal ladder (similar to monkey bars on a playground). Most of us could stay aloft for only a few bars before falling off. The Captain was enraged. "Pussies!" he shouted. In Vietnam, he said, he saw soldiers trying to cross a jungle river by hanging onto a rope (that had been stretched across the river) and moving hand over hand, but some of the men—weighed down by full packs and rifles—weren't strong enough to hold onto the rope, and they fell off and drowned in the river. "They drowned like rats!" he shouted. "Like rats! You weaklings better come out here at night and work on these bars."

# 5

# Sleep Deprivation

Our day began at 4:30. We had 45 minutes in which to shave, dress, and make our bunks. At 5:15, we fell into formation on the company street for the morning PT. We ran on dirt roads for several miles, up and down hills, in total darkness. A good runner was posted 10 yards in front of each platoon with a flashlight to alert approaching vehicles. At 6:15, we returned to the company area for more PT. We had to race through a series of exercises—horizontal ladder, run-dodge-and-jump, low crawl, push-ups, and pull-ups—on our way to the mess hall, and if anyone slacked off, he didn't get to eat breakfast.

The rest of the day was filled with exercise, instruction, and menial chores (such as picking up cigarette butts and pine needles), all accompanied by incessant shouting and insults. We were called a variety of disparaging names, including shitheads, assholes, pussies, scumbags, slimeballs, pansies, and queers. One verbally clever sergeant would refer to a poorly performing trainee as a "sad sack of shit" or "an idiotic turd," or he would tell him that "whale shit is at the bottom of the ocean, and you're lower than whale shit." (I don't want to leave the impression that all Army sergeants were foul-mouthed. At another unit after basic, I encountered a Mormon sergeant whose strongest words were "I'm as mad as h-e-double-toothpicks.")

At night, we got little sleep. We were supposed to go to bed at 10:00, but as things turned out, we were up until 12:30, which meant that we got only four hours of sleep. Each night we would go through the same deceptive routine. At 10:00, the official time for "lights out," we would turn off all lights, slip out of our boots, and get under the covers. Like clockwork a lieutenant in a jeep would drive down the company road, stop in front of each barracks, walk inside, shine a flashlight around to make sure all men were in their bunks, walk out, get in his jeep, and drive to the next barracks. As soon as he was out of sight, we would get up, turn the lights back on, and continue our chores. We had to do this because we had much work to do to satisfy requirements for shined boots and spotless barracks, and we didn't want to be punished the next day for deficiencies.

Why did the lieutenant come around each night? I later learned that it was part of the Army's attempt to solve a chronic problem. When trainees in basic training didn't get enough sleep, they wrote about it in letters home. Distressed by the reports, some parents complained to their senators and members of Congress, who then pressed the Army on why it failed to let trainees get enough sleep. The Army responded by requiring an officer to visit each barracks right after lights out, and then sign a log verifying that lights were out.

All of the men in our platoon cooperated in the fakery—except Gupton. Instead of pretending to be asleep and then getting up when the lights were turned back on, he would doze off immediately. Some of the men would angrily yell at him and drag him out of his bunk. He seemed dazed and confused.

Because we got only four hours of sleep each night, we were drowsy much of the time, especially when we were crammed into bleachers, sweaty and grouchy, to listen to a lecture. The instructor usually spent half the period trying to keep us from snoozing. He would make us stand up frequently to scream our company chant, "Bravo! Bravo! Bravo!" Or he would make everyone jostle the man on either side of him with hard elbow jabs.

One sergeant sometimes caught nappers with a little trick. In the course of his talk, he would say, in a normal voice, "If you're awake, don't pay attention to this command: ON YOUR FEET!" Those asleep would jerk to attention, blink at their laughing comrades, then sit down with a sheepish expression on their faces.

Another sergeant had a clever way to make everyone stay awake. The first man he caught napping was required to hold a gas grenade. (It contained CS gas and was used in Vietnam to drive Viet Cong out of tunnels. It didn't kill, but it did cause coughing, difficulty breathing, and burning of eyes, nose, and throat.) The sergeant made the trainee keep a tight grip, so that the safety lever was held firmly against the body of the grenade, and then he yanked the pin. As long as the trainee held on tight, we were safe. The sergeant told us that if he caught another man sleeping, he would take the grenade from the first man and make the new offender hold it. This announcement prompted my platoon mates to yell at me and Flewellen to keep Gupton awake. They obviously distrusted Gupton's ability to keep the grenade from spewing gas. So Flewellen and I sat on either side of him and kept a close watch and nudged him whenever he seemed ready to nod off. If the sergeant's goal was to keep us awake, he succeeded, but if his goal was to have us retain what he was teaching, he failed. We were too fixated on the grenade to absorb much of what he said.

On some nights, we didn't even get four hours of sleep. If we had to pull fireguard duty, we would spend one hour patrolling inside and outside the barracks, watching for fire. Then we would wake up our replacement. Fire was a serious concern because the barracks were old and wooden, and most of the men smoked. Although there were butt disposal cans on each floor, painted red, with an inch of water in the bottom, there was fear of careless handling of matches, lighters, and cigarettes. Another potential source of fire was the barracks' furnace room, which had a coal-burning furnace to heat water for our showers. Sergeant Boone never assigned Gupton to fireguard duty because he feared he would be too inept to keep the platoon safe.

Because we were terribly sleep-deprived, we welcomed the one day out of seven when we could catch up on our sleep. Sunday. Blessed Sunday. We could sleep late, but not too late—we had been tipped off by a trainee (who had a cousin who had recently gone through basic) that if you stayed in the barracks on Sunday, you risked being assigned to a work detail. For this reason, six or seven of us, including Flewellen, Gupton, and me, would spend much of the day in two places that permitted snoozing.

The first refuge was Sunday morning services at Harmony Church Chapel, where fortunately the chaplain made no effort to rouse us when we dozed off. The second refuge was the Special Services library for trainees, located near our barracks. After lunch, we would spend the afternoon sleeping in the air-conditioned building. The library was filled with trainees, all of them dozing, slumped in chairs or sprawled on the floors. I have always loved libraries, and the trainee library was astonishing. I would have expected old, dusty volumes, but the shelves were filled with a rich, eclectic, up-to-date selection of books and magazines on current events, science, and sports. There were literary masterpieces and the latest popular novels. The books were new and fresh and probably rarely opened. I hungered to devour good books, but my hunger for sleep was greater. I would get a promising book, read a few pages, and then fall asleep.

"The librarians are angels," I wrote in a letter to my fiancée. "They never yell at us to wake up. They let us slumber. It is absolutely quiet in the peaceful, air-conditioned oasis."

One evening I was summoned to the orderly room to talk to a company clerk, Spec 4 Townsend. (Spec 4 stands for specialist fourth class, a rank that is equivalent to corporal). He was working on a document that Captain Bosch planned to send to battalion headquarters—a "recommendation for discharge" aimed at sending Gupton home. Because I was Gupton's bunkmate, Townsend interviewed me for information about his deficiencies. He was glad to hear details such as Gupton's inability to make his bunk presentable for inspections.

Townsend and I became friends, and I would often go to the orderly room to chat with him on those evenings when he was on duty.

# 6

# Running Away

One night a member of the Muck Squad (who was from a different platoon) ran away. He was called Fat Boy by the sergeants, and he apparently couldn't tolerate the stress and harassment (I heard that his drill sergeant and platoon mates had taunted and hazed him mercilessly). On orders from Captain Bosch, a drill sergeant went out in his personal car to look for him. He was easily spotted and apprehended. Instead of being turned over to the MPs, he was returned to the barracks. The next day his entire platoon was punished for his going AWOL. They were required to perform extra PT—push-ups, sit-ups, and a two-mile run. To exact revenge, they gave him a blanket party that night. A blanket party is an old Army tradition whereby a blanket is thrown over a man during the night while he is lying in his bunk, and he is beaten by his tormenters, who are anonymous in the dark.

Warnings about AWOL were given throughout basic. We were shown Army films and given lectures informing us that going AWOL was cowardly and could hurt a man's chances of getting good jobs in the future. We were told that if a man ran away but turned himself in before 30 days were up, he was charged only with being AWOL. But if he were still running loose at the end of 30 days, his name was turned over to the FBI and the charge against him became desertion. In wartime, Captain Bosch warned us, a man could be shot for desertion.

Sergeant Boone asked me to keep a close eye on Gupton in case he tried to go AWOL. I agreed, but I laughed inwardly.

There was no way that Gupton could sneak out of the barracks, find his way out of the vastness of Fort Benning, and arrange for transportation to a safe haven.

The subject of going AWOL came up in one of my conversations in the orderly room with Spec 4 Townsend. I learned that Captain Bosch wanted to get rid of as many members of the Muck Squad as possible because they threatened to pull down the company average on the end-of-basic tests. Then why, I asked, didn't the Captain just let Fat Boy go AWOL and not try to apprehend him? For that matter, why didn't the Captain harass the rest of the Muck Squad viciously until we broke down and went AWOL? Townsend explained that the Army was experiencing a major manpower shortage because thousands of soldiers were running away, so it was doing everything possible to discourage AWOL, including holding officers and sergeants responsible. If you were a commander, and one of your men went AWOL, it was a mark against you. Bottom line: the Captain wanted to get rid of Muck Squad members, but not via AWOL.

After Fat Boy was given his blanket party, I saw him when he lined up for a Muck Squad run. He had purple bruises on his face, and his eyes showed fear and desperation. The Captain taunted him by saying, "If you ever go AWOL again, you're gonna get another ass whipping!"

During my time in the Army, I observed that some officers and sergeants tolerated (and sometimes even encouraged) scapegoating of men who were "different"—overweight or dimwitted or inept—but Sergeant Boone never allowed men in our platoon to victimize the unfortunate. Whenever there was grumbling about Gupton or any other trainee who was struggling, Sergeant Boone counseled restraint. During a water break one afternoon, some of the men complained that Gupton failed to do his share of the platoon's chores. The Sergeant replied that Gupton "never should have been drafted," adding that he was sure he would be sent home. I admired Sergeant Boone because he was tough and demanding, but also fair and understanding if a trainee faltered while trying to do his best.

Although some trainees complained about the blandness of Army food, one man who loved it was Johnny Gupton. He liked being able to eat three big, hearty meals every day. Because of his scrawny physique, I suspected that he had lacked access to lots of food back home. Army meals were generous. At breakfast, for example, we could go through a serving line and choose any or all of the following: sausage, bacon, eggs, grits, dry cereal and milk, a banana, an orange, pancakes and syrup, toast and jelly, orange juice, coffee, and milk. I knew a few other men in the Army who had come from deprived backgrounds and were ravenously happy to get three generous meals a day. In the mess hall, Gupton would shovel down his food, and if I had any leftovers, he would gobble them, too. Sometimes, after dinner, a commercial food truck would cruise through the company, and Flewellen and I would buy Gupton some snacks such as hamburgers, candy bars, or ice cream, which he would immediately wolf down, even if he had just finished a big meal. As the weeks went by, he gained weight, and he eventually lost the gaunt, emaciated appearance that I had seen when I met him in Nashville.

We were supposed to take a 20-question written test every week on what we had learned, but to save time, the chore was done for us by a trainee appointed by Sergeant Boone. The trainee filled in the answers so that the tests had different mistakes, with grades ranging from 80 to 100. Then the tests were passed out to us and we signed our name on whichever test was handed to us. On one occasion Gupton (who couldn't read) was given a test with a grade of 95. He signed his name by putting an X in the signature blank. I got a score of 80 when

I knew I could have made 100. I was irritated—not because Gupton outscored me, but because I had spent too much time in college to be satisfied with a B when I deserved an A.

One Saturday our platoon was given a couple of hours of free time, so Flewellen and I joined several other men, including Gupton, in walking to the PX. Giddy over being released from stress and chores, we sang marching songs we had learned in basic, including this one, which was sung to the tune of the "Colonel Bogey March" in the film *The Bridge on the River Kwai*:

*Hitler had only one big ball,*
*Goering had two but very small,*
*Himmler had something simmler,*
*But Goebbels had no balls at all!*

Like most Americans who grew up in the 50's and 60's, we knew about Hitler and his henchmen, and we made jokes about Hitler's manhood. Everyone laughed—except Gupton, who seemed unable to comprehend the humor. One platoon mate asked him, "Do you know who Hitler was?"

Gupton shook his head.

In the pre-cellphone days of 1967, our communications with the outside world were limited to the U.S. mail and telephone calls on weekend evenings at pay booths near the company. A happy event in our lives was mail call in the evenings, when we would gather around the mail clerk to discover if we had received a letter. I enjoyed reading love letters from my fiancée. (Later in our Army days, we could receive packages of cookies or candy, but in basic, no goodie boxes were allowed.) At every mail call, Gupton would stand with the rest of us, but he never received anything.

One night in the orderly room, Spec 4 Townsend informed me that Captain Bosch's request for a discharge for Gupton had been turned down by battalion headquarters. This rejection prompted the Captain to request that Gupton be sent to Special Training Company, a unit that gave extra training to men who had failed basic training. But this request was also denied because there was a rule that a trainee couldn't be sent to Special Training until he failed the final tests at the end of basic (or unless he was injured and needed rehabilitation). Without this rule, Townsend said, Special Training would be swamped with problematic trainees that commanders wanted to get rid of.

# 7

# The Sergeants' Great Fear

After a lot of marching and running with our rifles, we finally got a chance to go to the rifle range and fire them. But before we fired our first shot, a rifle-training sergeant, who knew that some men feared that the rifle would have a vicious kick, gave us a demonstration to show that the M-14's recoil was harmless if we held the rifle firmly against the body. First, he held the butt of the rifle against his stomach and fired. No problem. Then he held the butt against his chin and fired. He didn't flinch. Then came the supreme test, designed to convince any remaining skeptics. He held the rifle against his groin and fired. Again, no ill effects.

The fear of recoil was gone for most of us, but Gupton and a few others never got over their fear of the weapon, and they closed their eyes and flinched every time they pulled the trigger, ensuring that their shots were off-target.

Firing an Army rifle might seem like an easy task. After all, don't you just point it and pull the trigger? No, it's more complex than that. We had to align the sights, hold the rifle steady, breathe correctly, and gently squeeze the trigger without flinching. Our target was sometimes close and sometimes far away—and the varying distances required different strategies (for example, we had to aim high for some distances, and aim low for other distances). The M-14 had a 20-round magazine, and we had to know how to take out one magazine and insert another. We had to know how to disassemble the rifle, clean it, and then put it back together. For all of these tasks, Gupton was too slow-witted and confused to succeed. On the rifle range, he struck fear in the hearts of the sergeants because he was clumsy and uncoordinated, and he handled the rifle in a careless, sloppy manner. The sergeants feared that he would accidentally shoot someone.

We learned how to fire from various positions—kneeling, squatting, standing, and prone. The most uncomfortable position was the squat, with our feet flat on the ground (we were discouraged from crouching on the balls of our feet, like a baseball catcher). Sergeant Boone made us practice squatting, because he said the Viet Cong had a big advantage over us. "They squat every day of their lives and it's easy for them. While you're sitting in a chair, they're over there squatting." The squat was important because it was the best position in a rice paddy—you stayed low, yet your rifle and ammunition did not get wet. Gupton had trouble with the squat. Whenever he crouched down or tried to stand up, he would wave his rifle erratically—another source of fear for the sergeants.

For a week or so, a sergeant was assigned to accompany Gupton at the rifle range. I overheard the sergeant telling other sergeants that Gupton should absolutely *never* be allowed to handle loaded weapons on his own. All the sergeants agreed that big trouble would happen in the weeks ahead when we trainees simulated combat with such maneuvers as "fire and movement," in which you advanced in parallel lines with a partner through an assault course. While your partner ran ahead, you provided covering fire. Then he dropped to the ground and provided covering fire for you as you ran ahead. And so on, down the field. The sergeants foresaw disaster. Even scarier, for them, was the thought of what might happen in a few weeks when we would throw live grenades.

In the orderly room one evening, Spec 4 Townsend told me that Captain Bosch was trying once again to have Gupton discharged. A memo that was prepared for battalion headquarters described Gupton's ineptitude with firearms and warned that he presented "a grave danger" to the lives of trainees, NCOs, and officers. Townsend and I agreed that the new memo made a powerful argument for sending Gupton home.

Convinced that Gupton would soon depart, Captain Bosch stopped sending him to the rifle range and instead assigned him to daily KP—"kitchen police"—which was a harder job than it sounded. Most men hated the duty because you worked 16 straight hours, peeling potatoes, sweeping and polishing floors, cleaning tables and sinks, scouring pots and pans, and washing dishes and kitchen utensils in a hot, steamy kitchen. But Gupton seemed not to mind. I think he took some comfort in being in a place where he could perform the duties well and not be yelled at as much. And of course he was near his much-desired food. Men on KP were allowed to eat before the rest of the company arrived, and they could eat as much as they wanted. I heard that the mess steward viewed Gupton as a hard worker and liked having him in his kitchen.

Every morning, Flewellen and I would make sure he was up at 4:30. We would guide him to quickly shower and shave and get dressed, so that he could be at the mess hall by 5:00. We would not see him again until 9 p.m.


A week after Gupton began his daily KP duty, word came from battalion headquarters that Captain Bosch's latest effort to get rid of him had failed. According to Spec 4 Townsend, the Captain was furious, stomping around the orderly room yelling obscenities. Townsend also said the sergeants who worked in the orderly room were worried that they might get in trouble because they were required each day to sign documents certifying that each man in the company had completed various requirements, such as learning first-aid and throwing a live grenade. When Gupton was put on permanent KP, these sergeants falsely listed him as having completed the necessary training out in the field. Now they feared that they could be court-martialed for falsifying Army documents.

At some point, according to Townsend, the Captain calmed down, and he told the sergeants not to worry. He said he had a plan for Gupton, and "everything's gonna be okay." He stopped all his efforts to have Gupton moved out of Bravo Company.

Townsend said that some of the sergeants were dubious about the Captain's plan—whatever it might be—because they believed that a day of reckoning would surely come. After all, you could keep Gupton from the rifle range, but at the end of basic, he would have to demonstrate his marksmanship abilities on the final rifle test. The sergeants could cheat on the day-to-day records, but they couldn't cheat on the final test. Why? Townsend explained that there were three tests a trainee had to pass in order to graduate from basic training: (1) rifle marksmanship, (2) G-3 proficiency on what we had learned in basic, and (3) a PT test measuring our physical fitness. "In the old days," said Townsend, some company commanders would falsify scores on the tests in order to make themselves and their men look good, so the Army changed the system. All trainees were now required to take the tests under impartial training cadre at an official testing center.

In my talks with Townsend, he freely bad-mouthed the Captain, referring to him as "loony" and "a nutcase." What surprised me was that he would make disparaging remarks even if a lieutenant or a sergeant were present. I asked him if he was afraid that his insulting words would be reported to the Captain, and he replied that all of the lieutenants and sergeants were afraid of the Captain, but "he doesn't scare me." He said that if the Captain found out about the insults, there was no serious retribution that he could inflict.

"No serious retribution" referred to one of the harshest punishments that a superior could inflict during the Vietnam

War—transferring a man to an infantry platoon in the war zone. In the case of Townsend, he had already served a year in Vietnam and was due to be discharged from the Army a few weeks after Bravo Company graduated. Army policy dictated that if a man had served a year in Vietnam, he could not be sent back against his will. This policy created two vastly different types of non-career soldiers. In the first group were men who had not yet gone to Vietnam. They tended to be uptight and obedient, not wanting to displease a superior and risk being sent into combat. In the second group were men who had served in Vietnam for a year. They tended to be loose and unafraid. Their attitude about possible reprimands and punishments was often expressed by a shrug of the shoulders and the sarcastic statement, "What are they gonna do, send me to Vietnam?"

# 8

# Hearing Voices

Soon after Captain Bosch abandoned his efforts to get rid of Gupton, he launched a campaign to get rid of another member of the Muck Squad—a trainee named Murdoch, who was in a different platoon. Murdoch was weird, hearing voices that no one else heard. He was unfazed by the dictatorial authority of his superiors. When officers or sergeants screamed at him for failing to act or speak correctly, he would give them a blank look and say something that had only a slight connection to what was being discussed. For example, one day when the Muck Squad was assembled, Captain Bosch noticed stubble on his chin and growled, "Did you shave this morning?"

Rather than yes or no, Murdoch replied with a rambling jumble of pronouncements about body odor and his belief that the sergeants were stealing his soap and shaving cream.

At first, Captain Bosch suspected that Murdoch was faking insanity in order to be discharged from the Army. But as time went on, he got weirder and weirder. I heard that he would lie in his bunk and talk to an imaginary person.

Finally the Captain became convinced that Murdoch was insane, and he tried to get him removed. Spec 4 Townsend showed me some of the memos that the Captain had sent to battalion headquarters. But as with Gupton, battalion leaders were resistant to any request that would deplete the number of men in the battalion.

Then one day, suddenly, Murdoch was gone. But not in a way that anyone had foreseen. Spec 4 Townsend told me that Murdoch's drill sergeant had dispatched him to battalion headquarters to borrow an electric buffer (for polishing floors) because the platoon's buffer was not working. The sergeant had assumed that Murdoch would walk in and ask a clerk for permission to borrow a buffer. Instead, Murdoch wandered around in battalion headquarters until he found the biggest office, which belonged to the battalion commander. He walked in without knocking or saluting or seeking permission to speak, and asked the commander—a lieutenant colonel—for a buffer. The commander was taken aback by Murdoch's casual manner and his total lack of deference and fear in the presence of a high-ranking superior. To make matters worse, Murdoch proceeded to play with a miniature cannon and other memorabilia on the commander's desk—an astonishing invasion of the officer's personal space and property. As the commander questioned Murdoch, he observed the trainee's weird and illogical responses. At first suspecting that Murdoch was playing some kind of joke on him, he summoned other officers to witness what was happening. One of his aides told him that Murdoch was the man that Bravo Company had been trying to have discharged for being crazy.

The commander immediately arranged for Murdoch to go to Martin Army Hospital, where he was evaluated by a psychiatrist, who concluded that he was not faking. He was diagnosed as having schizophrenia, confined in the hospital, and eventually sent home with a medical discharge.

In conversations with some of his platoon mates, I was told that Murdoch had seemed normal at the beginning of basic training, but that stress and fear in basic had caused him to "go crazy." (To seek clarification, I later queried several psychiatrists, who pointed out that schizophrenia is a disease that can lie dormant during childhood and then explode into psychosis in adulthood, especially if there is a trigger such as extreme stress. The psychiatrists pointed out that stress in basic training could not create schizophrenia, but it could act as a trigger for someone who had a latent form of the disease.)

Captain Bosch, according to Spec 4 Townsend, was happy to see the departure of a member of the Muck Squad.


For several days, Gupton told me and Flewellen, "My teeth is killin' me." We tried to get him to go on sick call, but he declined because he was afraid that some of his teeth would be pulled. Finally, Flewellen got permission from Sergeant Boone to accompany Gupton to see a dentist. When they returned, Flewellen gave me a full report: It turned out that two of Gupton's teeth were abscessed and had to be removed. As he sat in the dental chair, he was extremely fearful, especially when the dentist used a scary long syringe to numb his mouth with Novocaine. (This procedure, as it was practiced in the 1960s, was quite painful.) When the dentist asked him if he had ever been to a dentist before, Gupton answered no.

# 9

# Two Varieties of Hell

Captain Bosch intensified the afternoon runs, driving us relentlessly in the brutal, muggy Georgia heat. Neighboring companies prudently did their runs in the mornings, but Captain Bosch said we had to be prepared for the heat of the jungles of Vietnam. I tried hard but I would straggle behind the company every afternoon, along with several other men. My head would get feverish and my throat would feel parched. Something hot and sour would churn furiously inside my stomach. About five minutes after I stopped, I would get intense cramps in both stomach and shoulders. I sometimes vomited. I got weaker and weaker, and after what happened to a platoon mate named Mitchell, I grew more and more afraid of collapsing on a run.

Mitchell was a bit overweight but for some reason, he had been overlooked in the selection of members of the Muck Squad. He was, however, destined to score low on the PT test. One steamy, hot afternoon, he collapsed during a run with our platoon, and when he failed to get up, the Captain ordered the drill sergeant of the platoon behind us to run his men over him. Run over him they did, breaking his ankle. He was sent to the hospital and that was the last the company saw of him. Later, Spec 4 Townsend told me that the Captain was pleased to see Mitchell go, because that meant one less weakling to pull down the company average on the final PT test.

The next day, as the company ran in the heat and humidity, I straggled behind, feeling weak and dizzy. I staggered to the side of the road and sat down under a tree. I was afraid of collapsing, as Mitchell had done. I was terrified that if I collapsed, I might crack my head on the road, or get stomped by other trainees, or fall under the wheels of a passing truck. I had decided that if I felt close to collapsing, I would do everything possible to be off the road when it happened.

I reached for my canteen and was getting ready to take a swig of water when Captain Bosch bore down on me. He grabbed my canteen and emptied the water on the ground. "You goddamn pussy!" he roared. "Get back up and run like a man." I got up and staggered down the road.

The next afternoon, as we trudged through the Georgia countryside to the rifle range, the air was unbearably muggy. We were the only company to hike out. Trainees from other companies jeered at our misfortune as they rode by in trucks. The trucks stirred up long billows of dust, which we had to swallow. My mouth was dry, and my rifle and pack bore down heavily on my back. I was drenched in sweat, but the sweat had little cooling effect because the air was too humid to permit much evaporation.

After we marched an hour or so, I got heat cramps in my shoulders and became dizzy and nauseated. At one rest stop, I took a swig of water from my canteen, which made me vomit. Flewellen came over and felt my forehead, which he said was burning up. He summoned Sergeant Boone, who splashed cool water on my face. Then, to lighten my load, the Sergeant carried my rifle, while Flewellen carried my pack, and we continued our march. When we arrived at the rifle range, I felt sick and dizzy and I walked to a patch of grass, lay down, and blanked out.

The next thing I knew I was in an ambulance, headed toward the hospital. A medic was taking my temperature, which was 105. When I got to the hospital, my temperature was still 105. I was stripped down and dunked in a big hospital tub filled with ice and water. God, it hurt! I cried out in pain, and fought to get out. Two medics pinned me down and another stuck a thermometer into my mouth. For 20 minutes, they pinned me down. Finally, when my temperature had dropped five degrees, I was allowed to get out. What relief! My teeth chattered as I dried off and put on hospital pajamas. Then I was led to a bed.

Later in the day, a physician reviewed my record and interviewed me, and he said I was lucky to be alive. He said I had been suffering from progressive heat illness and I was in danger of a heat stroke, which he said could have been fatal.

The next day I wrote a letter to my fiancée and I mentioned that "I once read somewhere that in ancient times, people in desert lands imagined hell as extremely hot, a place of eternal flames, while people in frigid northern climates imagined hell as a place of ice and bitter cold. Yesterday, I went through both kinds of hell."

I was kept in the hospital for a few days, and then released to go back to Bravo Company. But while I was gone, Captain Bosch had secured permission to have me sent to Special Training Company because I had missed key days of training and needed "rehabilitation" before being recycled to another basic training company.

Spec 4 Townsend picked me up at the hospital to take me to Special Training, but first we stopped at Bravo to collect my belongings. I wanted to say goodbye to Gupton, and I asked if I could go to the mess hall, but I was told that there was not enough time. Because Gupton couldn't read, I dashed off a farewell note to my buddy Flewellen and asked him to tell Gupton "goodbye and good luck." I put the note on Flewellen's bunk, picked up my duffle bag, and headed out.

As we drove to Special Training, Townsend told me that Captain Bosch was happy to get rid of me. "You're lucky to be leaving," he said. "The Captain's a certified nut—he'll do anything to win a goddamn trophy, even if it means hurting his own men."

I assumed that Gupton would fail basic and join me at Special Training Company, but he never appeared. I found out why a few weeks later when I talked to Flewellen, who had just graduated from Bravo Company and stopped by Special Training to visit me. Captain Bosch had devised a clever plan to raise the company average on all three final tests—PT, rifle, and G-3 (general knowledge). On the day before the tests, he ordered the younger-looking sergeants to have their heads shaved by a barber so that they looked like trainees. Right before each test, the company's "weaklings, fatties, and dummies" (as Captain Bosch called them) were hidden in an empty barracks, where they took off their fatigue shirts and gave them to the sergeants. In this way, each sergeant wore a shirt with a sewn-on name tag that matched the name on an individual scorecard. Needless to say, the sergeants made high scores, turning trainees who were losers into winners—at least on official records.

The Captain's ruse jacked up the company average, but it meant that in Gupton's personnel file, he would stand out as a bright and athletic soldier and an expert with the M-14 rifle. When I heard the news, my first thought was that his impressive test scores would probably enhance his chances of being assigned to infantry in Vietnam. But I hoped that somewhere along the line, his deficiencies would be noticed and he would be sent home.

In the years after Fort Benning, I tried periodically to contact Gupton, without success. As I prepared this book, I did some intensive searching, and I was surprised to discover that he had spent a year in Vietnam. I could not get many details, but I did locate a man who had served as a lieutenant in the transportation company to which Gupton was assigned. This veteran did not remember much about Gupton except that he was protected by a friendly sergeant, who had grown up with a "mentally handicapped" sister and was sensitive to his plight. The sergeant gave Gupton menial jobs, including KP, and kept him from dangerous assignments. I consulted the death records of the Office of Vital Records of the Tennessee Department of Health and found that Gupton died in 2002 at age 57.

As for Captain Bosch, he achieved his goal of having Bravo Company win a trophy for best training company in the battalion. Spec 4 Townsend had told me that Bosch hoped someday to become a general, and I am sure he felt that his achievements at Bravo Company would benefit his quest for glory.

But he never made general. As I gathered information for this book, I came across Bosch's obituary. After his stint at Fort Benning, he returned to Vietnam for two more tours of duty, and he stayed in the Army until he retired with the rank of lieutenant colonel. He died in 2011 at age 74.

Part Two

# *Special Training Company*

# 10

# Joe Tucker's Bad Back

When I arrived at Special Training Company, I was taken to the orderly room to be interviewed by the first sergeant. Undoubtedly influenced by my goofy face, he said, "We gotta fill out some paperwork—can you read and write?"

"I hope so," I said. "I'm a college graduate." He gave me a surprised look. He was just one of many who prejudged me because I appeared to be a dolt. I smiled and said, "I bet you thought I was one of McNamara's Morons."

He grinned. "We've got a lot of morons here. We don't need any more."

When I told him I wanted to pass through Special Training and finish basic as quickly as possible, he seemed pleased, and we ended up having a friendly conversation.

There were about 100 men at Special Training, most of whom had failed basic training because they possessed one or more of these attributes: mentally slow, weak, inept, overweight, or psychologically troubled. Also present were trainees who were convalescing from injuries, including Mitchell, the trainee whose ankle had been broken in Bravo Company. He hobbled about in a cast, waiting for healing and then assignment to a new basic training company.

Whereas physical training occupied about 40 percent of our activities in basic training, it consumed 90 percent in Special Training Company. We were supposed to get instruction that would help us with the rifle test and the G-3 proficiency test, but there was very little assistance. Low-IQ men were supposed to get remedial reading lessons, but I saw no evidence of such training. At Special Training, it was PT all day, every day (except Sunday).

After I stowed my gear in a wall locker, I joined the company, which was on the PT field struggling with the most excruciating physical torment I have ever endured in my life—intensive log drills. Each log was a 14-foot section of a telephone pole. Assigned to a group of six men, we had to hoist the log onto our shoulders, and then walk and run with it, and do exercises, such as bending over, holding it above our heads, or shifting it from one shoulder to the other. Frequently we couldn't maintain our hold on the log, especially if several men sagged their shoulders, and the log would fall, sometimes hitting a leg or foot. Whenever I underwent this ordeal, my back and shoulders would ache for hours afterwards, and I feared that I would suffer a hernia or a grievous back injury.

The drill was nothing but torture, involving no true rehabilitation or strengthening. If "torture" seems too strong a term, consider that when members of the Armed Forces are sentenced to "hard labor" at military prisons, they are obliged to undergo log drills. (The Navy's Safety Center warns prison officials that "log drills are inherently dangerous, and failure to adhere to the proper procedures can result in serious injury or death.")[1]

Log drills were not part of any tests in basic training—I had never encountered them until I arrived at Special Training Company. If you look at the faces in Figures 1 and 2, you can imagine the pain involved. If robust Marine recruits struggle, and if a Navy SEAL grimaces, you can see how agonizing it was for the weaklings at Special Training.

Figure 1. U.S. Marine recruits struggle to lift a section of a telephone pole in recruit training in San Diego.

Figure 2. A Navy SEAL grimaces as he lifts a log during drills.

We had log drills at least once during the day and then, in the evenings, anyone who had displeased a sergeant was forced to undergo post-dinner log drills.

During a water break one day, I expressed—in a friendly way—my concerns to several sergeants, pointing out that the log drills were tearing us down instead of building us up. The sergeants admitted that the log drills did not build our strength. They said the company commander had been ordered to make the drills as painful as possible to discourage malingering. Because a trainee was not supposed to be sent on to advanced training (and ultimately Vietnam) until he passed basic, commanders suspected that some men might fake an inability to pass the PT test so that they could spend the remainder of their Army time at Special Training instead of in Vietnam. The sergeants said that the pain of log drills had caused more than one malingerer to quit pretending to be weak.

One suspected malingerer was a trainee named Osborne, who said that he had injured his back in log drills. He limped all the time, and claimed that he was in extreme pain. The sergeants goaded him and accused him of faking. On the PT field, he groaned and winced, and he walked and ran like a cripple.

For several days I observed him closely, and I noticed that he seemed to be in pain even during those private moments when a malingerer might have relaxed—for example, when he was on the toilet or climbing into his bunk or bending over to tie his boots. Because of my rapport with the first sergeant, I went to him and told him I thought Osborne was not faking, and I recommended that instead of a routine visit to sick call (where he would be given a couple of aspirin and sent back to training), he should be sent to the hospital for examination.

The next morning a sergeant came into the barracks and told Osborne that he was being taken to the hospital for an exam. Several of us gathered around him to wish him well. "I hope you can go home," I said.

Joe Tucker, a low-IQ trainee, overheard this, and after Osborne had departed, he asked me if Osborne was going home. I explained that he was going to the hospital for an exam, and I felt that he would probably get a medical discharge and go home. (It took a few weeks, but Osborne did indeed get a medical discharge.)

Tucker failed to process my word "probably" and kept saying, with a tone of amazement, "He's goin' home... he's goin' home." Tucker was weak in mind and body, but unlike many of the low-IQ men, he was not meek or subdued. He was perpetually angry and aggrieved, and he talked back to the sergeants. When they cursed him and threatened him, he would say angrily, "I just wanna go home! Why don't you let me go home?"

An hour after Osborne's departure, we began our physical training, and Tucker suddenly developed a severe back pain. He groaned and moaned and told the sergeants that his back was killing him. The sergeants sneered at his malingering and shouted at him to stop faking. But he persisted in displaying a pretty good imitation of Osborne's pain and limping.

"You're a goddamn malingerer!" snarled one sergeant.

"I ain't no maringer," snapped Tucker. He not only mispronounced the word, but I am sure he had no idea what it meant.

When it came time for our lunch break, Tucker did something that surprised everyone. After a morning of limping and wailing, the moment we were dismissed, he forgot all about his bad back and raced to the mess hall to try to be first in line. The sergeants laughed and shook their heads in disbelief. During lunch, some of the sergeants came by Tucker's table and asked, with feigned solicitude, if his back was still hurting.

After lunch, we resumed our physical training, and Tucker resumed his back-pain charade—until a company clerk came and escorted him to the office of the company commander,

Captain Brown. About thirty minutes later, Tucker returned to the PT field, and he was a changed man. No more limping and wailing. Now he was enthusiastic and eager.

During a water break, I asked him what had happened.

"I'm goin' home," he said gleefully.

"What?"

"Yessiree, the Cap'n tole me, if I work hard and pass that dad-blamed test, he'll let me go home."

His enthusiasm lasted an hour or so longer, as we progressed through a practice PT test. Unfortunately, he was woefully slow and inept, and it became obvious that he would never pass. He lost his enthusiasm and returned to his angry, aggrieved demeanor.

By the way, Captain Brown did not lie. I found out that he promised Tucker that if he passed the PT test, he could go home *on a weekend pass*. This was a qualifier that Tucker failed to grasp, but it didn't matter. Enthusiastic or not, he could never pass the test. The only thing the captain achieved was to cause Tucker to forget about his "bad back." There were no more charades.

# 11

# Not by Strength Alone

Again and again, the men of Special Training Company were required to practice taking the Physical Combat Proficiency Test, and again and again, most of the men flunked it with abysmally low scores. So, the solution was for all the men to work hard to strengthen their bodies, right?

Wrong. While the PT test was an assessment of *physical* strength, you needed more than muscle to pass it—you also needed at least a moderate level of *mental* competence, which most of the men lacked.

To pass the test, you had to score at least 300 points out of a possible 500. There were five events, so you were encouraged to strive for at least 60 points in each event (although you were allowed to go below 60 in one event if you could make up the deficit in another event).

The first event was the low crawl, which looked easy. You crawled on dirt or sand as fast as you could for 40 yards. But there was a catch: instead of crawling on your hands and knees like a baby, you had to hug the ground as if you were sliding beneath enemy bullets or barbed wire, with your chest and belly pressed against the earth. The only acceptable way to propel yourself forward was by clawing with your hands and pushing with your feet, a hard way to gain any speed. To get the minimum of 60 points, you had to finish in 36 seconds. (See Figure 3.)

Figure 3. Soldiers at Fort Bliss, Texas, in 1972 demonstrate the correct way to perform the low crawl, with chest and belly on the ground.

Most of the men failed to get any points at all because they were disqualified for getting up on their knees. They had trouble grasping the concept of keeping their trunks against the ground and moving forward like supple lizards.

The second event was the horizontal ladder, a series of overhead bars that you traversed by swinging from rung to rung. You were supposed to go the entire length, turn around, and come back to the starting point. At first glance, the ladder looked identical to the monkey bars often seen in children's playgrounds, but there was a significant difference: each rung turned freely in its mounting, causing some men to spin off unless they swung quickly to the next rung. (See Figure 4.)

The biggest mistake made by most of the men was relying on strength alone. They would hang like dead weight from the first rung, and then proceed slowly and painfully to the next. They spent most of their time and energy in trying to hold on—until they lost their grip and dropped off. To achieve the minimum of 60 points, you had to negotiate 36 rungs before one minute elapsed. Most of the Special Training men dropped off after three or four bars.

Figure 4. The horizontal ladder required speed as well as strength. Photo shows a soldier in an infantry company at Fort Bliss, Texas, in 1972.

Though I wasn't strong and muscular, I traversed the 36 rungs in under one minute—much to the amazement of many onlookers. My success was due to a mental imaging trick I had learned from a sergeant in basic training. One evening I took some of the men to the ladder to try to teach them the trick. I explained that they needed speed as much as they needed strength. Instead of hanging from each bar as dead weight, they should move quickly—to maintain forward momentum. "A sergeant taught me to imagine that I'm an ape swinging quickly from branch to branch," I told them. "Even if one hand slips off a branch, I've got enough momentum to grab the next branch and keep going." Then I demonstrated the technique, and invited them to try it. Unfortunately, none of the men were able to translate the idea into action.

The third event was the run-dodge-and-jump. Running a zigzag course, you had to dodge wooden obstacles as if you were a nimble football player sidestepping would-be tacklers, then jump a shallow ditch. To get the minimum score of 60, you had to make two round trips in 25 seconds. (See Figure 5.)

Some of the Special Training men were befuddled by one aspect of the course: the wooden obstacles had directional arrows, and if you failed to go in the right direction, you were disqualified. A person of normal intelligence would observe the arrows ahead of time and run in the right direction without pausing or breaking stride. But these men would hesitate in order to study the arrows and think about which way to go. For each second they paused, they lost 10 points. A few of the men were unable to jump across the ditch, so they were disqualified.

Figure 5. The run-dodge-and-jump required agility and quickness.

The fourth event was the grenade throw. You were supposed to hurl five non-explosive training grenades 90 feet onto a huge canvas target which was flat on the ground and resembled a giant dart board. The scoring was similar to that of a dart board, too—the closer you came to the bull's eye, the more points you got. In order to simulate combat conditions, you were required to stay on one knee while throwing. Until you got the knack of it, it was hard to stay on one knee and still get your body weight behind a throw. Most of the Special Training men were too weak or uncoordinated to come close to the target, so they got a zero. (See Figure 6.)

Figure 6. A soldier at Fort Bliss demonstrates the required posture for throwing a grenade.

Committing a major mistake, the men tried to throw the grenade in a straight line. It was too heavy to permit such a technique. In one practice session, a sergeant tried to create a mental image: Don't throw the grenade like a baseball pitcher throwing to the catcher. Instead, throw in a high arc, like a centerfielder throwing a ball toward home plate. But the men couldn't understand what he was driving at, or else they couldn't translate it into action. Their throws were pathetic little trajectories.

In basic training, I had always scored very high—despite being unathletic—because I used the recommended posture and just reared back and threw the grenade as hard as I could, a method that happened to be perfect for hitting the bull's eye. Unlike stronger men, I didn't have to do any calibration of how hard to throw. In the first practice test I took at Special Training, a sergeant stood on the bull's eye as a way of taunting the trainees, knowing that no one could come close to hitting him. When I launched my grenade, it headed straight toward him. Caught off guard, he jumped out of the way at the last moment, and my grenade landed on the bull's eye.

"Goddamn!" he said. "What the hell are you doing in Special Training?" For a weakling like me, it was one of the most delicious triumphs of a lifetime.

The fifth event was the mile run. You were required to wear heavy combat boots, which caused you to run slower than if you were wearing sneakers. To get the minimum of 60 points, you had to complete the run in eight minutes, 33 seconds. (See Figure 7.)

Figure 7. In the mile run, combat boots were required. These soldiers were taking part in a PT test at Fort Bliss in 1972.

To succeed in the mile run, you obviously needed endurance, but you also needed problem-solving ability. At the beginning, some of the men would sprint as if they were running a 100-yard dash. This caused them to become out-of-breath and tired, and they would slow down and struggle for the rest of the mile. They couldn't grasp or apply what the sergeants told them about the need to maintain a steady pace (not too slow, not too fast) throughout the entire mile.

For most of the men in Special Training, passing the test was impossible. Their low mental capacity doomed them to failure. They could *never* pass. Under military rules, they were supposed to stay at Special Training until they passed all requirements for graduation from basic. So what was going to happen to them? Would the Army keep them in the company until their service time came to an end? Or would they be discharged and sent home? Or—horrible to imagine—would there be cheating (of the kind that Captain Bosch had used in Bravo Company) to send them on to Vietnam?

# 12

# "I Refuse to Train!"

While most of the men did poorly on the PT test because they were limited mentally, this was not the case with Charles Lassiter, who was very intelligent, but too weak and clumsy to pass. He was about 6' 1" and had long, spindly legs, and yet he was unable to jump across the ditch in the run-dodge-and-jump. When he ran through the course, he took short, dainty steps, and he was too uncoordinated to make the leap.

There was something about Lassiter that elicited fierce hatred from the sergeants. They hounded him constantly, calling him a "queer" and a "pansy." During the training day, he was screamed at more than anyone else, and in the evenings, he was always given log drills as punishment.

Finally, he couldn't take it anymore. At lunchtime one day, he sat on his bunk and declined to fall out for afternoon formation. I tried to coax him into getting up, but he said "I can't take any more of this shit." He seemed deeply depressed. A sergeant appeared and ordered him to join the company, but he refused. The sergeant fetched the company commander, Captain Brown, who gave him a direct order to get off the bunk and join the company on the PT field. (In the military, refusing to obey a direct order given by a commissioned officer is a serious crime that can result in harsh punishment.)

Again, Lassiter refused. The MPs were summoned, and they arrested him and took him to the stockade. We never saw him again. (I heard later that he was court-martialed and sentenced to four years at hard labor in the military prison at Fort Leavenworth, Kansas.)

As we stood in formation on the PT field, one of the sergeants announced, in a taunting, triumphant voice, "Lassiter has refused to train, so the MPs have taken him to the stockade. Anyone want to join him?"

Like a flash, Joe Tucker cried out, "I do!"

"You refuse to train?"

"Yes!"

I interjected, "Sergeant, he doesn't know what he's talking about."

The sergeant told Tucker, "Say it if you mean it— 'I refuse to train.'"

"I refuse to train."

"Say it louder."

"I REFUSE TO TRAIN!"

"Okay, buddy boy," said the Sergeant, grabbing his collar and hustling him to the orderly room.

Not long afterwards, Tucker returned to the PT field with his customary scowl, and he silently rejoined us. I found out later that Captain Brown had explained to him that the word "stockade" meant jail, and that saying "I refuse to train" would result in a trip to jail, not a trip home.


Lassiter's refusal to train must have caught the attention of high-ranking officers at Fort Benning because a few days after the event, a "full bird" colonel visited the company. Captain Brown assembled us in front of the colonel and said that we were fortunate to have him with us because he was a combat veteran of World War II, and he had important things to say to us.

The colonel proceeded to give us a motivational talk. He was a white-haired, distinguished-looking officer, and he seemed sincere and concerned. Without making any reference to Lassiter's deed, he exhorted us to fulfill our duties and fight to guarantee the liberties enjoyed by our families and friends. Our nation was involved in a conflict between the forces of freedom and the forces of darkness. Insidious, totalitarian communists wanted to enslave us and trample upon our rights. We must be strong men, obedient men, and we must be willing to sacrifice, like Washington's troops did at Valley Forge in the darkest days of the Revolutionary War, like Eisenhower's troops did on the beaches of Normandy.

He continued in this vein, and as he spoke, I glanced at the men near me. They were looking at the speaker respectfully, but I knew that most of them were not comprehending his concepts. It was a bit comical, as well as a bit sad. Here was a well-meaning World War II veteran who seemed unaware of the intelligence level of most of his listeners, talking about patriotism and other abstractions to men who had no idea of what he was talking about.

Despite Lassiter's refusal to train and Joe Tucker's dream of going home, there were a few men at Special Training who seemed content to be in the Army. One of them was Willie Smith, a black trainee from Mississippi. He was big and muscular, with broad shoulders and huge, powerful arms. The sergeants thought he was faking his inability to pass the PT test because of the common stereotype of the muscular black as (almost by definition) a good athlete. He received a great deal of verbal abuse from sergeants—both white and black—who assumed that he was a malingerer.

He was very strong in lifting heavy objects, such as the telephone poles in log drills. Whenever we had log drills, the rest of us tried to get on his team because we knew he could shoulder more than his share of the load. What gave him trouble was any event that required agility and quickness. For example, on the horizontal ladder, he stayed aloft the entire one minute allowed, but he negotiated only 8 or 9 bars. He had the strength to hold on to each bar and avoid slipping off, but he failed to move swiftly from one rung to the next.

One day he told me about growing up in a rural area with little money and no car, no TV, not even a radio. He was amazed at the Army's largesse. They gave him two beautiful pairs of boots and a wardrobe of clothes, including a snazzy, dress-green uniform—all free. They served him three bountiful meals a day—free. Moreover (he could hardly believe it) there was *meat* with every meal. (At home he was lucky to get meat twice a week. He said that growing up, he had subsisted mainly on buttermilk and potatoes). In the Army, if he became ill or got a blister on his toe, he could go to a doctor—free. If he got a toothache, he could go to a dentist—free. And once a month they gave him $95 spending money. He considered himself lucky.

Another man who considered himself lucky was Lemuel Simpson, a small, frail man of limited intelligence. Nervous and high-strung, he scurried about furiously, trying his best to please the sergeants so that they wouldn't scold him. Because he was obsessive about doing his duties correctly, he was often assigned to unpleasant tasks like cleaning toilets. He would work hard to make them shine.

I learned that Simpson had been the butt of a terrible practical joke in his basic training company—so terrible that he was forced to leave the company after only three weeks. (The story was told to me by two of Simpson's friends from his old platoon. They had worried about him and visited him one Sunday. As they were leaving, I pulled them aside and asked them what had happened.) It seems that one afternoon Simpson was summoned by his drill sergeants to the garbage cans behind the mess hall. The whole company was witnessing the scene. One of the sergeants told Simpson that there was a pussy cat hiding behind the garbage cans, and his assignment was to go behind the cans and catch her. Ever eager to please, the little fellow dutifully went after the cat.

The cat turned out to be a skunk, which bit him and sprayed him. He spent the next two weeks in the hospital, getting doses of vaccine injected into the muscles of his abdomen, a painful prophylaxis which was necessary to head off the possibility of rabies.

I talked to him one evening about the skunk, and he was not bitter about the incident. He had no idea that the sergeants had played a trick on him. He even saw a bright side to the skunk's attack: his clothes had to be destroyed and as a consequence, he got a brand-new set of fatigues, cap, underwear, socks, and boots. Lucky guy!

In the evenings, I would often help men write letters home. I remember one trainee who was dictating a letter to his mother, and he gushed about how happy he was that the Army had given him a pair of glasses. "I can see people's faces real good now," he said. He apparently was unaware of his vision deficiency until the Army tested him and prescribed glasses.

# 13

# The Ugly Young

As I noted earlier, the sergeants tried to make life hard for all of us because they wanted to weed out any malingerers. While I was at Special Training, I knew of only one man who admitted to faking. A new arrival, Jeff Hardin, boasted in the barracks that he had deliberately failed the final PT test in basic training so that he would come to Special Training and not have to go to Vietnam.

Hardin was a tough guy, who said he entered the Army because a judge had given him a choice: join the Army or go to jail. He bragged about his record of crime, including aggravated assault, breaking and entering, public drunkenness, and resisting arrest. He said he had been in and out of many jails.

Either tipped off about his malingering or sensing his game, the sergeants harassed him ferociously. They yelled at him constantly and made him perform endless exercises. At first, he maintained his tough guy persona and appeared not to be bothered. "It's better than being in Vietnam," he would say in the barracks. But the sergeants finally punctured his shield of invincibility, and—no surprise—the instrument of their success was log drills. Every evening, he would be assigned to interminable log drills, along with other men who had misbehaved or in some way displeased the sergeants. After a few days of agony, Hardin went to the first sergeant, confessed his fakery, and asked to take the PT test. He got permission to take the test with a regular basic training company so that he could quickly exit from Special Training.

After he passed the test with a high score, he returned to Special Training to wait for orders that would allow him to depart for advanced training. I was standing with a dozen or so other trainees in the shade next to the barracks when he joined us and bragged about his success. "I'll take my chances at the next place," he said.

Then, without any provocation, he started jeering at us. "I'm glad to get away from you guys. McNamara's Morons! Look at you—you're the ugliest, sorriest asses I've ever seen."

He walked from man to man, hurling insults. To one man, he said, "You've got buckteeth and big thick glasses. It hurts my eyes just to look at you."

To another, he said, "You're so fat, you're disgusting. No girl would ever want to touch you."

I finally had enough of his crap. I told him, "We're all trying to do the best we can. We don't deserve ridicule and contempt."

He looked me up and down, and sneered, "Well, Mister Know-it-all, you may be a college graduate, but you look like a fuckin' reetard."

I wanted to give him a withering retort, but I couldn't think of anything to say. (Of course, in the days and years to come, I would think of all kinds of clever comebacks. Too late.)

It was true that most of us were unimpressive physical specimens—overweight or scrawny or just plain unhealthy-looking, with unappealing faces and awkward ways of walking and running. In a letter to my fiancée, I showed off with some fancy prose, describing Special Training men as "the ugly young: the glum faces and misshapen bodies you see hunched on benches late at night in a Greyhound bus station."

Hardin was not the only man to jeer at us. Sometimes trainees from other companies, riding by in trucks, would hoot at us and shout "morons!" and "dummies!" Once, when a platoon marched by, the sergeant led the men in singing,

*If I had a low IQ,*
*I'd be Special Training, too!*

(It was sung to the tune of the famous Jody songs, as in "Ain't no use in goin' home/Jody's got your girl and gone.")

One exception to the general unattractiveness was Freddie Hensley. Even though all his hair had been shaved off by an Army barber, he was a good-looking young man, with a fresh, appealing face. One sergeant called him "Pretty Boy." This was the first impression of Freddie. On second glance, however, there was something amiss. His eyes were chronically filled with apprehension and self-doubt. Like some people who are consumed with dread and anxiety, he was always sighing. If I were sitting on my bunk and he approached from behind me, I could hear him coming. He was a veritable sighing machine.

One day Freddie and I and several other men were chosen to go to the rifle range to see if we could qualify with the M-14 rifle. Sending men to the rifle range was a rare event for Special Training because it was considered unnecessary for most of the trainees. You had to pass the PT test before you were sent to the rifle test, and since most of the Special Training men were unlikely to ever pass the PT test, why waste time in rifle training? Freddie and I and the other men who had been selected were considered exceptional—we were expected to pass through Special Training quickly and move on down the road to Vietnam.

We went to the rifle range with a sergeant who was supposed to coach us. Freddie knew the correct technique for holding and firing the M-14, and if given plenty of time and a conventional bull's eye to aim at, he could hit the target. But the marksmanship test wasn't given with fixed targets. Instead, to simulate combat conditions, pop-up targets were spread out on a brushy hillside, ranging from 50 meters to 350 meters in front of the firer. You never knew when and where a target would pop up, and each target stayed up just a few seconds.

*Here's one to the right at 50 meters. Freddie takes careful aim, fires. BLAM! But he's too late. The target is gone. Now one silently pops up on the left at 200 meters. Freddie doesn't see it until a few seconds have elapsed. By the time he gets it in his sights, it's gone. He doesn't fire a single shot. "Wake up!" the sergeant screams. "Get your head outa your asshole!" A target pops up straight ahead at 300 meters. Rattled by the sergeant, Freddie impulsively raises his rifle, and without taking careful aim, he fires. Misses it. Fires again, misses again. "Goddammit!" screams the sergeant. "Control your aim!"*

The rest of the test was much the same. Freddie was simply too slow to pass. At first I wondered why Freddie had been chosen to take the rifle test, but it soon dawned on me that he was selected because he was a handsome young man. Many people equate good looks with competence, and ugliness with incompetence. Freddie didn't *look* like a dim bulb. (I must confess that I was slow in realizing his mental limitations. It seemed to go against the laws of nature for a good-looking lad to have an intellectual disability.)

In addition to being slow, Freddie also was ignorant of some basic facts. There was a thunderstorm one afternoon, and we were ordered to wait in the barracks until the threat of lightning diminished. As Freddie and I sat together on foot lockers and looked out the window, I passed the time by trying to figure how close the lightning was. I counted the number of seconds between a lightning flash and the subsequent clap of thunder. (Five seconds equals one mile.) I tried to explain what I was doing, and I was not surprised that Freddie could not comprehend. What *was* surprising was my discovery that Freddie did not know that lightning caused thunder. He knew what lightning was, and he knew what thunder was, but he did not know that one caused the other.

# 14

# Sent by God?

For natural athletes, a military obstacle course is pure delight. You squirm under barbed wire, climb over hurdles, swing on a rope across a stream, scramble over fences, crawl through tunnels, and walk a narrow log across a gulley. (See Figure 8.) A well-trained platoon looks powerful and aggressive as it goes through a course: spirited, robust males leaping and climbing and clawing their way to the finish line. Most of Special Training Company's men, in contrast, were clumsy, uncoordinated weaklings struggling against daunting obstacles.

The most hated part of the course was the rope swing. You were supposed to grab a rope at the top of an embankment and swing down to low ground on the other side of a shallow stream. Most of the men couldn't hold on to the rope long enough, so they landed in the water or in the mud next to the water.

The next obstacle was a concrete drainage pipe, which we were supposed to crawl through quickly. It was about 15 yards long, and it went through the base of a hillock. One afternoon a sergeant caught a trainee trying to bypass the obstacle without being observed. The sergeant grabbed him by the shirt and pushed him down to the ground at the mouth of the pipe.

Figure 8. Crossing over a barrier is a common task in a military obstacle course. This photo shows airmen at an Air Force obstacle course at Camp Guernsey, Wyoming.

The trainee, who was extremely overweight, screamed, "I caint do it!" He began to cry.

The sergeant was incensed. "You big fat crybaby!"

One trainee, Bill Tarkenton, spoke up, telling the sergeant that the man was scared of getting trapped in the pipe. He asked for permission to help him.

The sergeant assented, and Tarkenton got down on his hands and knees next to the trainee. In a friendly, patient voice, he promised the man that he would not get trapped inside the pipe. "See that patch of light at the end of the tunnel? Keep looking at that light—if you see that light, you know it's not sealed off." He said he would be at the end of the pipe and not let anyone block it off.

Trembling with fright, the trainee entered the pipe, as Tarkenton spoke to him from the other end, giving him encouragement and reassurance. When he emerged from the pipe, he was shaking all over and his face was wet with tears. Several of us gathered around him, clapping him on the back and offering congratulations.

This incident was typical of the kindness of Bill Tarkenton, the only man in the company who had more education than I had. He was a law school graduate, a married man, and a member of the Nebraska National Guard. When he finished basic training, he was scheduled to return to Nebraska, assume the rank of captain, and serve as an attorney in the Judge Advocate General's Corps.

Several men who had been at Special Training for many months idolized Tarkenton. Before he arrived at Special Training, I was told, it was common for some sergeants to steal money from the men—by demanding donations to fictitious groups such as "the wounded soldiers' fund" or by "borrowing" money and never returning it. A few sergeants would even beat recalcitrant trainees. But Tarkenton's mere presence put a stop to the abuse. The sergeants realized that he had the legal savvy to go through the chain of command to have wrongdoers punished. And the sergeants could not use a potent weapon often employed against would-be whistleblowers—the threat of sending a "troublemaker" to infantry in Vietnam.

Tarkenton had difficulty passing the PT test, but even if he never passed it, he would still go home when his National Guard active-duty stint was over in a few weeks. Lassiter, before he was sent to the stockade, told me that he believed that Tarkenton could pass the PT test whenever he wanted to, but that he chose to fail "because God sent him here to help us."

Whether sent by God or not, Tarkenton helped many men by counseling them and comforting them in times of stress and anguish. He was a gentle, soft-spoken man who possessed a quiet moral authority.

# 15

# "I Want to Know Why"

After a few weeks at Special Training, I took the final PT test and passed it easily. I was recycled to a new company to pick up where I had left off with Bravo Company. It was early autumn now, and it was exhilarating to be healthy and free of heat exhaustion and worries about passing out. I joined my new comrades as they were going on bivouac in the countryside. In a letter to my fiancée, I wrote, "It was a brisk autumn day today, and I enjoyed the training very much—charging through the woods with bayonets on our rifles, hungrily opening our little cans of C-rations, trudging like disciplined ghosts on the roadside for endless miles at night."

I finished basic training with my new company, and then I went to the U.S. Army Intelligence School at Fort Holabird in Baltimore, Maryland. While I was there, I happened to run into a man who had been at Special Training as a convalescent while he recuperated from a hand injury. He informed me that all of the men I had known at Special Training had been "administratively passed" and sent on to advanced training. He said the company commander had been ordered to certify that the men were malingerers who could have passed the final tests if they had truly wanted to.

I was stunned. This meant that Freddie Hensley and Joe Tucker and the other low-ability men might be in the pipeline to Vietnam. I feared that because they had supposedly graduated from basic training, there would be nothing to keep them out of combat.

I shared this fear with my informant, and he said that a sergeant had told him that McNamara's Morons would *never* get sent into combat. The sergeant was quoted as saying, "How long you think you'd live if you went out on patrol with one of those dummies?" I did not believe a word of it. If the Army was capable of "graduating" the men from basic and sending them on down the line, it was capable of sending them into combat.

While I was at Fort Holabird, I wrote letters and made telephone calls to the offices of members of Congress, protesting the "administrative passing" of low-IQ men and arguing that they should be barred from serving in combat. I was utterly unable to elicit any interest.

After Intelligence School, I went to Vietnam, but I had no contact with Project 100,000 men because I served as an Army intelligence agent. Wearing civilian clothes and using a fake name, I posed as a journalist, and I worked on a team that recruited and trained agents for espionage missions in Cambodia, a country from which communist forces launched attacks on American forces.

While I was in Vietnam, I continued to write letters to members of Congress, and I had one moment of success. An aide to Senator Robert Kennedy wrote me that he was moved by my descriptions of low-IQ men and was urging the senator to hold a hearing on Project 100,000. I eagerly watched the mail for a letter detailing plans by Senator Kennedy. But one morning in June, 1968, I heard the news that Kennedy had been assassinated. I suspected that my only chance for Congressional action had died with the senator. I was correct.

After I left Vietnam, I was stationed at Fort Meade, Maryland, and I spent my spare time visiting Congressional offices in nearby Washington, DC, to make my argument that Project 100,000 men should never be sent into a war zone. I rarely talked to a member of Congress or a senator—I was usually sent to talk to a low-level staffer or an intern. These individuals would listen politely, even make notes, but no action was ever taken. I concluded that I was just a poor persuader, but I eventually realized that I could get no action because low-ability men dwelt at the bottom of the economic ladder. They and their families had no political clout, so there was no Congressional interest in them. I should have seen this sooner. After all, it was their powerless political situation that had caused the men to be brought into the military in the first place.

A few years after the war ended, I arranged to get a computer printout listing all the names of Americans who died in Vietnam. I skimmed the list, looking for last names that matched the names of men I had known at Fort Benning. I expected to find Joe Tucker on the list, but he was not there. (I don't know whether he ever went to Vietnam, but if he did, he survived, because I later discovered that he died in his hometown in 2005 at age 57.) Unfortunately, the death list included the names of two men I had known at Special Training Company—Ernesto Lozano and Freddie Hensley. Lozano was a man I didn't know very well. The only thing I remembered about him was that some of the sergeants had given him the nickname Reetardo. Freddie Hensley, of course, I knew well. I was not surprised to discover that he had been killed in combat. With his good looks, he probably was assumed to be "normal" and was moved along to Vietnam and sent out into the field.

Freddie's death hit me hard. I remembered how he was always sighing—an indication of the tremendous anxiety he experienced in Special Training. I remembered how he lacked the mental quickness to qualify with the M-14 rifle. I felt enormous anger, which I still feel decades later. He never should have been drafted. He never should have been "administratively passed" at Special Training. He never should have been sent into combat.

Grasping at straws, I got to thinking that maybe there was another man named Freddie Hensley who died, so I tried to find his family by telephoning people in his hometown with the same last name. (This was in the days before the Internet, so finding people was more difficult than it is today.) I eventually made contact with his mother and ascertained that the Freddie I had known was indeed the man who died in Vietnam. I told her that I had been Freddie's friend at Fort Benning. She said that she and the family were proud that Freddie had given his life to defend his country. As we talked, I carefully introduced my belief that Freddie should not have been sent into combat. Before long, she was expressing grief and anger and bewilderment. She told me that when Freddie received his draft notice, she and other family members went to the induction center and explained that Freddie had been in EMR (educable mentally retarded) classes in school and had not been able to drive a car and that it would be a mistake to draft him. In response, a sergeant reassured the family that Freddie would not be put into danger—he would just do menial jobs such as sweeping floors and peeling potatoes.

"He was a good boy," she said. "When he was little, we used to go everywhere together. He was my Little Man." She began to sob, and she lamented, "Why did they have to draft him? I want to know why."

# Part Three

# *Project 100,000*

# 16

# Coercion

In the 17<sup>th</sup> century through the early 19<sup>th</sup> century, whenever the British navy had a shortage of sailors for its war vessels, it was authorized to practice impressment—sending "press gangs" into British seaports to round up able-bodied young men at random, immediately taking them to a ship and forcing them to become sailors. Men who resisted were executed.[2]

In the years before Americans won independence from Great Britain, some American men in seaports were included in the kidnappings. "Conditions in the naval service were horrible: bad food, backbreaking work, and brutal discipline," according to historian Alfred A. Cave. "Many victims of impressment did not survive the first year." From 1765 to 1775, anti-impressment riots broke out in American seaports, including Newport, Rhode Island; New York City; and Wilmington, North Carolina.[3] Even after the establishment of the United States, the British continued to impress U.S. sailors, kidnapping about 10,000 men from American ships between 1803 and 1812—an outrage that was one of the causes of the War of 1812 between the U.S. and Great Britain.[4]

The British were not the first to coerce men into military duty, nor were they the last. In the 20<sup>th</sup> century, the process was called conscription, or the draft, and it was carried out less crudely, with bureaucrats sending letters ordering men to report for duty on a certain date. The result, however, was the same: Young men were forced to leave their homes and enter the armed services.

Military leaders have never liked the idea of dragooning men into the ranks. They prefer to have warriors who are willing and eager to fight. Therefore, nations generally try to use persuasion to entice men to sign up, and rely on conscription only as a last resort.

When the U.S. government began to build up its troop levels in Vietnam in the early 1960s, it tried to fill the ranks with volunteers. TV commercials and magazine ads appealed to a young male's hunger for adventure and his desire to be transformed from a boy into a man. An Army ad in *Hot Rod Magazine* proclaimed "Vietnam: Hot, Wet, and Muddy—Here's the Place to Make a Man!"[5] For men without a job, ads stressed that the Armed Forces provided secure employment, adequate wages, and a chance for advancement.

In addition, government leaders gave speeches and interviews in an appeal to patriotism and fear. They argued that godless communists were trying to take over the world, and Americans needed to resist them in Southeast Asia and elsewhere before they landed on our shores.

Tens of thousands of men responded to the call and stepped forward to enlist, but their numbers were not large enough to satisfy manpower requirements. So the Selective Service System was used, as it had been in World War II and the Korean War, to draft young men.

(The focus of this book is on males because females were excluded from the draft, but it is worth noting that about 11,000 American women in the military, most of them nurses, volunteered for service in Vietnam, along with thousands of civilian women who served as doctors, nurses, journalists, missionaries, and workers for the Red Cross and other humanitarian organizations.[6] During the war years, 67 American women died in Vietnam—eight military nurses and 59 civilians.[7])

In 1964, at the beginning of the American troop buildup in Vietnam, the draft took relatively few men, but during the next seven years, as the American government escalated its troop levels in Vietnam, more and more men were needed.

For people who lived in the Vietnam era, it was a truism that the war did not enjoy wide popularity among young people. Today, however, some writers argue that the war was popular, citing the fact that the majority of Vietnam veterans were volunteers, not draftees. This, however, is a piece of information that is true but misleading. Yes, the majority of Americans who served in Vietnam were technically volunteers. Some were indeed true volunteers (such as the idealistic, patriotic youths described above), but most of them volunteered only because of the way that the draft was carried out. Local draft boards or military recruiters told them that they were likely to be drafted soon, and they had two choices: They could submit to the draft and serve two years, probably in combat. Or they could volunteer and serve three years in a non-combat MOS (military occupational specialty) such as truck mechanic, cook, or computer programmer. Most men chose the second, safer option. Because the vast majority of them would never have enlisted if the draft had not been in place, it would be more accurate to call them "draft-induced volunteers."

(I was in another category, which I call "draft-influenced volunteer." My local draft board put me on a list of possible draftees, but my family doctor told me—without any prompting on my part—that I could avoid the draft if he wrote a letter to the draft board about a pre-existing medical condition, hyperthyroidism. I declined his offer because the draft board's interest in me woke me out of my adolescent daze and forced me to take a hard look at the issues. Because I was a strong believer in America's fight against communism, I decided that it was my patriotic duty to serve, so I signed up for three years in the Army, with a promise of an interesting assignment—

military intelligence. But I make no claim to being a hero. I did not volunteer for infantry.)

During the major years of the Vietnam era (1964-73), there were 26,800,000 draft-age American males, 68 percent of whom never had to serve in the military. They were excused because they were students or fathers or had physical limitations or some other disqualifying status.

That left 32 percent to fill the ranks. Some signed up for hazardous duty, but the majority managed to steer clear of the battlefield by going into the National Guard or Reserves, which in the Vietnam War were rarely used for combat, or by signing up for non-combat positions in the Army, Air Force, Navy, or Coast Guard.[8] Some men spent their entire service time in non-lethal locales, such as the U.S., Germany, Korea, and the Panama Canal Zone.

Ultimately, out of every 100 American males of draft age in the Vietnam era, only 12 went to Vietnam. Of these 12 men, nine had non-combat support roles but weren't entirely risk-free (they were potential targets of rocket bombardments, booby traps, and terrorist attacks). The remaining three men served under fire in one of the following high-risk situations: (1) fighting in one of the hard-core combat arms of the Army or Marine Corps (infantry, artillery, armor, special operations, and close air support), (2) serving in dangerous positions in the Air Force, Navy, or Coast Guard (such as combat aviators or patrol boat warriors), or (3) trying to save lives in one of the most vulnerable of all battlefield jobs, combat medic.[9]

While a few men were eager for combat, most were not. Tony Zinni, a Vietnam veteran who later became a four-star general in the Marine Corps, said, "It was hard to find Americans who'd actually chosen to fight in Vietnam. Most who served there had been forced to go."[10]

# 17

# Avoidance

During the Vietnam War, almost all of the nation's affluent youth and a majority of middle-class youth escaped the draft by going to college or claiming a disability or exemption. This did not mean that all of the men who were excused from service were draft-dodgers. Some of them had legitimate medical conditions that made them unsuitable for military duty. Some were parents and could not be blamed for wanting to stay with their families. But a University of Notre Dame study estimated that 75% of excused men had actively tried to avoid the draft.[11]

If a young man wanted to avoid service, he could hope for help from one of the two components of the conscription process. First was his local draft board, consisting of civilians who could decide whether he qualified for a deferral (for being a college student, for example). If the draft board declined to let him off the hook, his second hope lay with the nearest induction center, which was run by the Armed Forces. After giving a pre-induction physical exam and an intelligence test, the induction center could excuse him for failing to meet physical or mental standards.

The goal for a draft avoider was to find a way out before he reached 26, the age at which draft boards stopped summoning men. In 1970, a board game called "Beat the Draft" was put on the market. In the game, a player tried to "move around a Day-Glo board picking up potential deferments, attempting to avoid Sergeant Jones at the Army's induction center. Reach the age of 26 and you're home free!"[12]

Throughout the war years, many loopholes were available. One of the most famous cases involved actor George Hamilton, who persuaded his draft board to give him a hardship deferment because he was the sole support of his mother, who lived in his Hollywood mansion and relied on his $200,000 annual income (which would be $1,375,000 in today's dollars).[13]

Men in certain occupations, such as engineers, farmers, teachers, ministers, and divinity students, won automatic exemptions.[14] Fatherhood could win a deferral, so a number of young men felt pressure to get married and start a family.[15] Years ago, a woman of my acquaintance mentioned her son— at that time, a high-school student—and said "he's my peace child," explaining that the boy was conceived at a time when Selective Service was edging towards taking the boy's father. The subsequent birth of the boy saved the father from being drafted.

A popular way to avoid the draft was to find a doctor who would attest to a medical problem, such as flat feet, extreme allergies, or skin rashes. While he was a student at Harvard, writer James Fallows recalls, "sympathetic medical students helped us search for disqualifying conditions that we, in our many years of good health, might have overlooked."[16] For $120, a young man could purchase a psychological disqualification. "There are reputable, antiwar psychiatrists who will put one through a series of personality tests to find some tendencies they can distort," a Harvard undergraduate explained in a letter home to his parents.[17]

Having a letter from a doctor was a sure way to win a medical exemption. For example, the induction center in Seattle, Washington, divided men into two groups—those who had letters from doctors, and those who did not. Everyone with a letter got an exemption, no matter what the letter said. Induction centers rarely had the time to contest what an outside expert said.[18] Using letters demonstrated the advantages held by middle-class men, who had easy access to a sympathetic physician. Working-class and poor men either had no such access, or they were unaware that a doctor's letter was an option.

Some men gained disqualifications by contriving to fail their pre-induction physical exams. A University of Michigan student ate three large pizzas each night for six months, so that he exceeded the military's weight limit for his height. He was disqualified.[19] Some men jabbed their arms with needles to pass themselves off as heroin addicts. "Desperate potential draftees," said the *New York Times*, "drank their own blood to feign ulcers and gorged on licorice stew because that was supposed to elevate blood pressure."[20]

Being under orthodontic care would win a disqualification. "Wearing braces," said Lawrence M. Baskir and William A. Strauss, "was a last-minute tactic for registrants who faced immediate call-up. According to one youth who wore unneeded braces, this 'dental cop-out' was 'very expensive and very uncomfortable. But it sure beat KP, getting up at 4 a.m., and going to Vietnam.'" In the Los Angeles area, "ten dentists willingly performed orthodontic work for anyone who could pay a $1,000 - $2,000 fee."[21] [In today's dollars, the range would be $7,000 - $14,000.]

Professional football players were virtually immune to being drafted. In 1966, Selective Service grabbed only two of 960 pro players, many of the rest finding refuge in the National Guard or Reserves. "We have an arrangement with the [Baltimore] Colts," Major General George Gelson Jr. of the Maryland National Guard said in 1966. "When they have a player with a military problem, they send him to us." The Dallas Cowboys had ten players assigned to the same National Guard division at one time.[22]

The most sensational football star of the era, New York Jets quarterback Joe Namath, was excused from service on grounds that his frequently injured knees made him unfit for combat. Yet he continued to play bone-crushing football on Sunday afternoons. (At Special Training Company, as we struggled with our physical challenges, my friend Bill Tarkenton and I would sarcastically comment on the fact that we had been deemed fit for combat, while superstar Namath was a reject, supposedly our physical inferior.)

If a young man refused to submit to the draft, he was subject to arrest and imprisonment. To escape this fate, over 40,000 American youths fled to countries that were willing to give them asylum, including Canada, Sweden, and France.[23]

About 171,000 men refused to submit to the draft because they were conscientious objectors whose religious or moral beliefs forbade them to kill in any war, or in the case of Vietnam, a war they considered unjust. Some of them were excused by local draft boards, while about 96,000 agreed to alternative service in such jobs as medics. An estimated 4,000 conscientious objectors were given long prison terms—usually five years.[24]

Some draft avoiders felt remorse over their actions. When he was 66 years old, film and TV actor John Lithgow revealed that while he was in his 20s, he won a disqualification by wearing urine-soaked clothes and pretending to be insane during a pre-induction interview. "A sense of shame," he said, "stayed with me for years and has never entirely disappeared. Some of that shame had to do with the appalling suffering caused by the Vietnam War, suffering that I so conveniently avoided."[25] Novelist Mark Helprin, in an address at West Point in 1992, told the cadets that during the Vietnam War, "I dodged the draft, and I was wrong. This is a regret that I will carry to my grave."[26]

Men who believed that the Vietnam War was a mistake could be expected to have no regrets, but it was surprising to see no regrets coming from draft avoiders who had been strong supporters of the war. One of my friends—who believed passionately that American forces should have continued the war until North Vietnam was crushed even if it meant that thousands more American soldiers would die—had no misgivings about sitting out the war. "My family spent thousands of dollars to put me through college and law school," he told me. "If I had joined the military and been killed in Vietnam, it would have been a waste of time and money." Former Vice President Dick Cheney, who spent the war in college and graduate school, sought and received five deferments from his draft board (four student deferments and one hardship deferment), even though he was pro-war. Years later, when he was one of the prime architects of the war in Iraq and was accused of being a hypocrite for sending thousands of men into combat, he justified his Vietnam-era behavior in this way: "I had other priorities in the '60s than military service. I don't regret the decisions I made."[27]

Reacting to comments by Cheney and other successful politicians, Paul Marx, a draftee in the Korean War, wrote in *The Baltimore Sun,* "For every draft avoider, someone else was made to serve in order to meet the military's quotas. That 'someone else' might very well have been killed in Vietnam. Many of America's most accomplished young men were ready to pass the buck and let someone else—someone less sophisticated and knowledgeable—make the sacrifices while they pursued their personal ambitions."[28]

Joining the National Guard or Reserves was a popular option because relatively few Guardsmen and Reservists were sent to Vietnam. Out of about one million men who enlisted in the National Guard and Reserves during the Vietnam era, only 15,000 of them actually served in Vietnam.[29] Alan Vanneman, who served in a combat artillery unit in Vietnam in 1968-69, said, "I trained with several hundred country boys from Louisiana and Alabama, who were bound for National Guard units. They were, as they gleefully put it, 'NG'— 'Not Going.'"[30]

When I was in college, some of my friends with political aspirations spoke frankly of how they wanted to avoid combat, but they didn't want to be denounced as cowards or draft-dodgers in future political campaigns. So they joined the National Guard or Reserves, and ended up getting military rank and honorable discharges that they could list in their biographies. Historian James E. Westheider describes how one future politician handled the matter: "George W. Bush said that he joined the Texas Air National Guard because 'I was not prepared to shoot my eardrum out with a shotgun in order to get a deferment. Nor was I willing to go to Canada.... So I chose to better myself by learning how to fly airplanes.'"[31]

Some men who avoided the draft would later become prominent leaders, such as Bill Clinton and Mitt Romney. But in fairness, it should be noted that a few young men who later became national leaders served in Vietnam and risked their lives. For example, three men who were members of the U.S. Senate at the same time—Chuck Hagel, John Kerry, and John McCain—were decorated heroes of combat in Vietnam.

Although some affluent men suffered in Vietnam, the typical infantry platoon was made up of minorities, the poor, and the working class, with a sprinkling of middle-class youth, according to Westheider.[32] San Antonio lawyer Maury Maverick Jr. recalled that during the war, "My friends at the local office of the American Friends Service Committee placed a cross on a map of San Antonio at the home address of each person killed in combat. On the West Side where the Mexican-Americans live, there was a sea of crosses. In Alamo Heights, Olmos Park and Terrell Hills, where the 'best people' live, there were virtually no crosses at all."[33]

Most of America's privileged elite seemed unbothered by the unfair burden placed on men on the lower rungs of society, but there were some leaders who were angry and indignant. In 1966, Kingman Brewster, president of Yale University, used his baccalaureate address to graduating seniors to denounce a system that drafted only "those who cannot hide in the endless catacombs of formal education."[34] In a similar vein, Congressman Charles Wilson of Texas said, "I believe that it is morally wrong for us to depend on the deprived and the unfortunate in our society to furnish the manpower for our country's Armed Forces."[35]

# 18

# McNamara's Plan

The year 1966 was crunch time for the American military. Because so many middle-class American males were avoiding the draft, the military faced the prospect of serious manpower shortages. The war in Vietnam was heating up and the American troop level there was nearing its peak of 543,000 men.

If the U.S. had sent 543,000 men to Vietnam in 1966 and kept them there until the war was over, there would have been no problem in meeting manpower needs. But the Pentagon had created a shortage by deciding that any man sent to a combat zone would not be required to stay longer than one year. Because most men did not volunteer to extend their tour of duty, thousands of fresh troops had to be deployed to Vietnam every month to replace the thousands that were departing.

Most of the troops inducted each month were volunteers and men who were drafted because they had no exemption or deferral (for example, high school graduates who did not go to college). But these men added together did not provide enough manpower to fill all the slots required in Vietnam.

To supply the extra troops that were urgently needed, President Johnson was faced with a tough choice. He could have revoked student deferments and forced thousands of college boys into the Army, or he could have used the one million men in the National Guard and Reserves. But either action would have angered the vote-powerful middle class, so he turned instead to the working class and the poor. Here, however, he also found trouble in rounding up enough eligible men. There were plenty of men of the right age in the poorer neighborhoods, but many of them had flunked the military's entrance exam—the Armed Forces Qualification Test (AFQT). Johnson and Defense Secretary McNamara desperately needed them, however, so they lowered the standards for passing the AFQT. Suddenly thousands of low-aptitude men, once declared unacceptable because of low AFQT scores, were now subject to the draft.

Johnson and McNamara tried to make their action appear to be based on humanitarian compassion. With much fanfare at the 1966 national convention of the Veterans of Foreign Wars, McNamara unveiled a plan to "salvage" and "rehabilitate" 100,000 substandard men each year—hence the official title, Project 100,000.[36] Called New Standards men, these disadvantaged youths—many from urban slums and rural poverty areas—would be molded into productive soldiers by being assigned to special training companies, which would be set up at each basic-training center to teach reading and arithmetic. Though the men may have failed these subjects in school, they wouldn't fail now because the military was "the world's greatest educator of skilled manpower." It knew how to motivate men and possessed an impressive array of pedagogical gadgetry. McNamara, once considered one of the most brilliant men in America (he had made a name for himself as one of the Whiz Kids who revitalized Ford Motor Company), believed that he could raise the intelligence of low-ability men through the use of videotapes and closed-circuit TV lessons. "A low-aptitude student," he said, "can use videotapes as an aid to his formal instruction and end by becoming as proficient as a high-aptitude student."[37]

This last statement prompted hoots of derision from many educators and psychologists, who knew the limitations of audiovisual instruction. In his starry-eyed belief that videotapes could dramatically transform slow learners, McNamara was revealing the same "blind faith in the power of technology" that deluded him into thinking that he could outsmart the enemy in Vietnam by using calculators, computers, and statistical analyses.[38] According to biographer Deborah Shapley, McNamara was "a naïve believer in technological miracles."[39]

In announcing Project 100,000, McNamara never said a word about combat. To hear him, one would have thought the men were going off not to war but to school. In his view, the military was doing them a favor. When they got out of the service, they would have valuable skills and self-confidence with which to get good-paying jobs in the civilian market.

Critics accused McNamara of cynically dreaming up Project 100,000 in order to disguise his true purpose: to use the poor instead of the middle-class for combat in Vietnam. The truth was more complex: McNamara had proposed Project 100,000 two years before the 1966 manpower crunch, seeing it as a way to contribute to the Johnson administration's War on Poverty. In fact, the idea had been kicking around Washington before McNamara arrived on the scene. Its leading advocate was Daniel Patrick Moynihan, a sociologist who later became a U.S. senator from New York, whose argument went like this: The best way to solve poverty in America was to draft the hundreds of thousands of young men being rejected annually as unfit for military service. Take inner-city blacks and poor, rural whites—both groups tending to be lazy and fond of booze—and put them into uniform. Instill discipline. Train them to bathe daily, salute, and take orders. Teach them a marketable skill. At the end of a couple of years, you will have transformed lazy, unmotivated slackers into hard-working, law-abiding citizens. Moreover, they will teach *their* children to be solid middle-class citizens, too, so that once and for all, you will have broken the generation-to-generation continuity of poverty.[40]

Moynihan's concept was embraced by both Johnson and McNamara in 1964—two years before Project 100,000 was launched. Secret White House tape recordings revealed a conversation in which Johnson said that he wished the military could be persuaded to take "second-class fellows," referring to men who had flunked the Armed Forces' mental test. If entrance standards could be lowered, Johnson told McNamara, the military would be the ideal place for a second-class man. "We'll teach him to get up at daylight and work till dark and shave and bathe," said Johnson. "And when we turn him out, we'll have him prepared at least to drive a truck or bakery wagon or stand at a gate [as a guard]." [41]

In response, McNamara told Johnson that uniformed officers in the Defense Department were opposed to drafting low-aptitude men because "they don't want to be in the business of dealing with 'morons' [in] 'moron camps.'... The Army doesn't want to be thought of as a rehabilitation agency."[42]

In 1964 - 65, Johnson and McNamara tried repeatedly to lower standards, but their efforts were successfully resisted by military leaders in the Pentagon and their allies in Congress. The powerful chairman of the Senate Armed Services Committee, Senator Richard Russell of Georgia, accused McNamara of trying to set up a "moron corps." The Department of the Army said it wanted to "fight with the highest caliber of men available."[43]

But then crunch time 1966 came along, and the top brass, desperate for manpower, had to capitulate: if Johnson and McNamara were not willing to draft a sufficient number of middle-class boys, then "second-class" servicemen would have to suffice. With bitter disappointment and grave doubts, military leaders went along with the decision of their civilian bosses, and Project 100,000 was instituted.

Between October 1, 1966, and December 31, 1971 (the official dates of the program), Project 100,000 took in some

354,000 men, 91 percent on the basis of lowered mental standards, the remaining nine percent because of less stringent physical standards (for example, men who had been deemed too heavy, too skinny, or too short were now accepted).[44]

Project 100,000 men were, on average, 20 years old. Half came from the South, and 41% were minorities.[45] Some 46 percent were draftees, while the remaining 54 percent were volunteers. However, as I pointed out earlier, the term "volunteer" is misleading. Military recruiters would get the names of low-scoring men who were now acceptable to the Armed Forces and visit them to steer them toward three-year hitches. The recruiters would tell them that if they waited for the draft, they would serve only two years but almost certainly end up in an infantry platoon in Vietnam. But if they signed up for three years, they would be assigned to a non-combat job. There was, however, a big catch: the military did not have to honor any oral promise made by a recruiter. A recruiter might promise a man a job like helicopter maintenance, but after basic training—when it was time to go to a specialized school—the military could decide that his test scores were not high enough to qualify for helicopter maintenance. Or in some cases, he could be sent to helicopter maintenance school and if he flunked the training, he was subject to transfer to infantry. Thousands of three-year Project 100,000 "volunteers" ended up in infantry because of this catch, which many critics denounced as fraudulent behavior on the part of the military.[46]

Project 100,000 men were assigned to all major branches of the Armed Forces—71% to the Army, 10% to the Marine Corps, 10% to the Navy, and 9% to the Air Force.

# 19

# "A Crime Against the Mentally Disabled"

While I was stationed at Fort Benning with men like Johnny Gupton in Bravo Company and Joe Tucker in Special Training Company, I wondered why in the world the military had inducted men of such low intelligence. How could they provide anything of value to the war effort?

In later research, I found out the reasons, and I discovered activities that were dishonorable, if not illegal.

To understand what happened, let's take a look at the Armed Forces Qualification Test (AFQT), which the military used to decide who was capable of learning military skills and who was not. The AFQT had 100 multiple-choice questions, and one hour was allowed. The questions started out easy and got progressively harder. Here is an example of an easy question in the arithmetic section:[47]

1. Bob wants to buy a wagon. He has 5 dollars and needs 5 dollars more. How much does the wagon cost?
   A. $10
   B. $15
   C. $25
   D. $55

An example of a harder question:

2. If 12 men are needed to run 4 machines, how many men are needed to run 20 machines?
   A. 24
   B. 48
   C. 60
   D. 80

For more examples of AFQT questions, see the Appendix in the back of this book.

Based on their test scores, potential recruits were divided into five categories, which corresponded to IQ levels.[48] (IQ—which stands for Intelligence Quotient—is a rough indicator of how well a person performs on intelligence tests in comparison to how his or her peers perform. Often criticized for being crude, shallow, and unfair, intelligence tests omit such important variables as creativity and intuition. Nevertheless, they are widely used as evaluation devices in education, business, and the military.)

Category I, very high IQ (124 and above)
Category II, above average IQ (108-123)
Category III, average IQ (92-107)
Category IV, below average IQ (72-91)
Category V, very low IQ (71 and below)

In the early 1960s, before Project 100,000 was launched, only men in Categories I, II, and III were considered to have the aptitude necessary for military duty, but when McNamara lowered standards, all men in Category IV and some in Category V were judged as possessing adequate mental abilities.

Because most of the men in Project 100,000 scored in the bottom two mental categories, does this mean that they were intellectually disabled or—to use the most common term of the 1960s—*mentally retarded?* No, the men were a mixed bag, as shown in an analysis of their categories:

Category IV, upper level—These men were close to having average intelligence, and they functioned fairly well in society and in the military. Some had "street smarts," able to perform well outside the classroom. They may have scored in Category IV not because of intellectual deficiencies, but because of limited schooling and poor test-taking skills. Some were successful in the military, as I will show in later chapters.

Category IV, middle to lower level—Many of these men would have been described in the civilian world as "slow" or "not very bright."[49] They—and the men in the category below them—were the ones most likely to be labeled as "McNamara's Morons" by their peers and by superiors.

Category V—Men scoring in this category possessed the lowest level of intelligence, and they were barred by an act of Congress from entering the ranks of the Armed Forces, *but some of them were taken nevertheless.* How did the military get away with what seemed like a violation of federal law? By employing a little-known loophole—called "administrative acceptance"— which was brought to light by writer Don Winter in an article in *National Journal.*[50]

"Administrative acceptance" meant that a man could be brought into the military despite a very low, Category V score. It was designed to snare draft-dodgers who were smart but pretended to be dumb on the AFQT. If a man was suspected of fakery, an examiner would interview him. If he had graduated from high school or had worked in a demanding job, he was deemed a faker, and he was administratively accepted, or—in many cases—he was told that he was a faker and that he would be administratively passed and sent into infantry unless he decided to take the test again and possibly qualify for a non-combat assignment. Usually the faker chose to take the test again and make a higher score.[51] For example, one man who was caught faking was a brilliant youth named Jamie Kelso of Los Angeles, who said, "I attempted to flunk the mental examination by figuring out the right answer on every question and answering incorrectly. That was a rather large boo-boo on my part. Of course I scored zero, and that was a statistical impossibility. A [trained] monkey who took the test and marked the A, B, C and D boxes [at random] would have scored twenty-five out of a hundred. The resident psychiatrist pointed this out and began threatening me [with combat duty in Vietnam]. So he sent me in for the mental test again. And I scored probably the first hundred they had ever seen there." (Kelso later used other means to escape induction.)[52]

If administrative acceptance had been used only to catch fakers like Kelso, there would have been no problem. But induction centers went further. Under the terms of the loophole, examiners and clerks were permitted to induct a man if they believed that he "possessed a higher mental level activity than was implied by test scores."[53] Here's how it played out: If an examiner or clerk felt that a Category V man possessed "street smarts" (common sense and shrewdness) that would enable him to perform well in the Army, he was inducted.

This elastic interpretation of the law infuriated David Robinson, a GI and veterans' counselor who observed the workings of the Houston, Texas, induction center during the Vietnam War. He said the majority of Category V men who were administratively accepted were neither fakers nor street-smart individuals, but men who were "truly deficient mentally."

"The process was a farce—highly subjective, grossly unfair, an outrageous abuse of the law," he told me. "A lot of men from the bottom of the barrel were accepted administratively just so that induction centers could ramp up the number of draftees for Vietnam."[54]

Robinson's accusation was backed up by Winter, who had discovered the loophole because "the day I was drafted—July

12, 1968—I was put to work in the Atlanta induction center screening AFQT scores." When he noted that clerks were placing the paperwork for mentally substandard Category V men in a stack of "administrative acceptees," he questioned the fairness and accuracy of their methods, but the clerks "shrugged off my questions: if there was any doubt, put 'em in the acceptable pile."[55]

Using administrative acceptance to draft Category V men was "a crime against the mentally disabled," said Robinson. "Most of the Category V men who were sent into the Army under administrative acceptance were truly disabled. But they never protested, they never complained. How could they? They were the lowest of the low, the dumbest of the dumb. They were being railroaded to Vietnam, and they never had a clue."[56]

Induction centers manipulated the rules because they were under intense pressure from the Pentagon to get as many men as possible into the military. By the end of the war, 30,301 administrative acceptees had been inducted.[57] Officially, they were counted as Category IV men, even though many of them—perhaps the majority—had IQs that should have placed them in Category V. But they couldn't be listed as Category V because Congress had decreed that anyone scoring in that category was "ineligible for service."[58]

Although induction centers fudged on categories, they did not fool government officials and veterans' counselors, who—in later years—were appalled when they discovered that some veterans "had mental test scores so low that they never should have been allowed in the military." These men were clearly in Category V, according to counselors at the Center for Veterans' Rights in Los Angeles, as well as William Strauss, an official on President Gerald Ford's Clemency Board.[59] Sociologist G. David Curry, an Army captain in Vietnam, also affirmed that "sometimes Category V men ended up on active duty."[60]

The question that I asked at Fort Benning—How did the military get away with taking men who had extremely low intelligence?—could be answered in this way: In many cases, the men were probably taken in through the administrative acceptance loophole. But there was another possible explanation—cheating by recruiters—which will be discussed later. Either of these explanations would account for the acceptance of men (like Johnny Gupton) who couldn't read and had mental liabilities but nevertheless "passed" the AFQT.

While many induction centers in big cities were using administrative acceptance to move Category V men into Category IV, one small, remote induction center in Anchorage, Alaska, was doing just the opposite. An Army enlisted man named George Buford was in charge of screening AFQT low-scorers. He cheated, but he did so for a noble purpose. "When I came across a Cat IV draftee who was within a few points of being a Cat V, it was a simple matter to make a few changes on his answer sheet and drop his score to Cat V, thereby make him draft-proof. I had no qualms about doing this.... I was able to keep a few of the mentally retarded out of the infantry and thereby out of combat; this not only saved their lives, it saved the lives of the infantrymen who would have died as a result of their bungling."[61]

The ease with which Buford changed test scores illustrated the power—for good and for bad—possessed by examiners and clerks.

# 20

# Sign up and See Paris

"My recruiter lied to me" is a statement I have heard many times over the years while chatting with Vietnam veterans. Here is a typical account of recruiter deception: In 1967, a man in New York City named Tony, who wore glasses, was told by his recruiter that "we don't send anybody to Vietnam who wears glasses" because the Army wanted men with good vision so that they could shoot effectively. So Tony signed on the dotted line, thinking that he would go to some non-combat place like Germany, and of course he ended up in Vietnam.[62]

George M. Watson, who served in the 101st Airborne Division in Vietnam in 1969-70, said that a World War II interpreter advised him "never to believe what anyone says in the Army unless you have it in writing, and then make several copies, sending one to your grandmother and another to your parents or anyone else you might trust for safekeeping.... What the Army respects is paper.... Always have it in writing."[63]

Recruiters had great success with recruiting for Project 100,000. As the war progressed, military recruitment of low-scoring men in poor urban neighborhoods "rose to an art form," says Myra MacPherson, a former *Washington Post* reporter and author of *Long Time Passing*, a major study of soldiers who served in Vietnam. As an example, she says that "black Marine Corps recruiters visited shabby slums where mothers were often fair game. Recruiters told them that if their sons were *drafted*, nine times out of ten they wouldn't get the job they wanted. But if their sons *enlisted* in the Marines, they would get 'valuable training.'"[64] Of course, the recruiters knew (but didn't say) that many of the young men, with their low AFQT scores, were unlikely to qualify for any training other than combat arms. They certainly could not qualify for the glamorous assignments—such as U.S. embassy guard in foreign countries—that were illustrated in the glossy brochures that recruiters gave to the mothers. One of the brochures said, "Paris is only one of the many overseas Marine Corps posts or installations where you could be stationed."[65]

The recruiting campaigns were very successful, says MacPherson. The large number of Project 100,000 volunteers from poverty areas in many cities "compensated for the decline in volunteers from more affluent neighborhoods."[66]

What if a young man could not read or write? Not to worry. Some Army and Marine recruiters used "ringers" (substitutes) to take the AFQT for candidates who could not pass the test on their own. Donald Robinette, a Marine recruiter, told a Congressional panel that ringers were used at the induction center in Cleveland, Ohio. He said that one of the ringers, who took the test for 15 different candidates, was so skilled that if you told him you needed a particular score—31, say—he would deliver the exact score.[67]

A brutal necessity for Army and Marine recruiters was meeting quotas. If they failed to sign up a certain number of men each month, they got poor evaluations from their superiors and risked being passed over for promotion. Marine Sergeant Kenneth Taylor, who was a recruiter for four years in the Detroit area, testified before a Congressional panel that the pressure of meeting monthly quotas was so intense, he and other recruiters cheated on mental, physical, and police-check (criminal record) requirements. For example, they supplied answers to intelligence tests or hired ringers to take tests for low-IQ recruits. Taylor's conscience bothered him. He felt guilty over the acceptance of "mental rejects" and other men who never should have been accepted in the Armed Forces. Finally, in an effort to call attention to the problems caused by the quota system, he took the unusual step of charging himself with "recruiter malpractice." He was punished with a letter of reprimand from his superior officer for "dereliction of duty," and he left the service with an honorable medical discharge for hypertension (high blood pressure), a condition that he blamed on the high stress of being a recruiter.[68]

Instead of putting enormous pressure on recruiters to meet their quotas, why didn't the military ease up on recruiting and just let the draft bring men in? Because some men, if they were left alone by recruiters, might not be drafted. They might fail to show up for induction or they might fail the mental tests (if they were graded accurately) or they might flunk the physical requirements (if they were applied honestly). For the military, the recruiters were vital because they could nudge and flatter (and make bright promises), and they could, if necessary, fudge the mental and physical tests. And of course if they signed up a man, he would serve three years instead of a draftee's two.

Recruiters often got help from induction centers. For example, in 1971 Terry Hughes of Buncombe County, North Carolina, went to the Charlotte induction center for pre-induction testing. "I told them I didn't want to go into the Army because I didn't like killing people. The sergeant who gave us the test, I asked him, 'If I fail it, will I have to go?' He said no. So I just sat there and filled in the answer sheet without looking at the questions. I thought sure I was free. But when I was going out of the room, he put my test on a pile without looking at it, smiled at me, and said, 'You passed.'" Hughes ended up in infantry and was sent to Vietnam. Fortunately for him, his plane landed on the day American combat involvement ended.[69]

Another induction center was quite accommodating, according to Mark Lloyd, who was a squad leader in a basic training platoon at Fort Lewis, Washington, in 1968. One "slow-witted" man in his squad was a Canadian who had failed the test to enter the Canadian army, so he came south to join the U.S. Army—which was no problem because "the Green Machine took anyone with a pulse." The Canadian "tried his best, but he had difficulty with the program. I spent an inordinate amount of time spoon-feeding the Army way to him. He sometimes had problems putting on his uniform. Often he would look at me with his open countenance while I helped correct his dress before morning inspection. Repeated mistakes in buttoning his shirt and putting on his equipment belt became frustrating. I reminded him every day he had to shower and shave—a new requirement for him. The Army training manuals, supposedly written for a sixth grader's comprehension, proved difficult for him. He improved little over the eight-week course, but he made it through the training. He went on to infantry, of course, as the infantry didn't care how well one could read. I still have our platoon photo, taken just before graduation, and there he is: standing in the last row, wearing that helpless expression on his face and his helmet on backward."[70]

The Canadian, incidentally, was an example of the kind of man I sometimes encountered in my research—a low-performing man who was not a draftee or a draft-induced volunteer, but a true volunteer who willingly signed up, often because of his inability to find a job in the civilian world.

Part Four

# *War in a Faraway Place*

## 21

# Training for War

To travel down the road to Vietnam, Project 100,000 men had to complete basic training (and in some cases, spend time at a special training company). Novelist Larry Heinemann, who served as an infantryman with the 25th Division in Vietnam, recalled that in his basic training barracks at Fort Polk, Louisiana, he would look across the street at McNamara's Men in a special training company. "These were the guys who simply could not hack it during regular basic training. It was painful to watch... some of them could not even get the hang of so simple a thing as standing at attention, and otherwise seemed severely unsuited for military life."[71]

Nevertheless, most Project 100,000 men were graduated from basic training, even if company commanders—like Captain Bosch in Bravo Company—had to cheat to get them through. For example, a veteran named Peter Hefron recalled a Project 100,000 inductee who had the mental capabilities of a 10-year-old. "He passed basic training because other soldiers in the unit used his ID card and took the necessary tests to get him qualified."[72] In other cases, trainees who failed were required to repeat basic training again and again, recalled one officer, until "we got most of them out and through the system."[73]

After leaving basic, Project 100,000 men went to AIT (advanced individual training) to learn infantry tactics, or if they were lucky, specialized skills such as radiotelephone operator. Some men performed well and succeeded in learning new skills, but others had problems in learning. Called the

"Moron Corps" at Fort Polk, Project 100,000 men "were pretty damn bad," recalled one officer. "Somebody had to help them get dressed in the morning.... They couldn't understand what was going on."[74] Another officer said, "Lots of these guys just weren't fit to do a job. I had to help one buy a toothbrush and pack his bags so he could report to another duty station."[75]

When McNamara launched Project 100,000 in 1966, he promised that the military would train the men in special skills that would lift them out of poverty.[76] Unfortunately "the promised training was never carried out," according to Christian G. Appy, a professor of history at the University of Massachusetts. There was simply no money available.[77]

"The real tragedy of Project 100,000," wrote Marine Captain David Anthony Dawson, "lay in McNamara's refusal to find additional funding for special training. McNamara announced that the services would take steps to modify their training for men with low test scores, but then he proposed budgets which allotted just enough to provide the minimum amount of training for all Marines. The Marine Corps could barely prepare men for combat. It had nothing left for remedial or vocational training."[78]

Yet remedial training was desperately needed. Drill Instructor Gregg Stoner was surprised that the Marine Corps was required to accept men who were "mentally slow" and unable to read. Many people, he said, might think that reading was unnecessary for Marine infantrymen, "but that was totally not true. If a Marine could not read, he couldn't tell what type of ammo was in the ammo box. He couldn't read basic instructions or orders."[79] Unfortunately, most Project 100,000 men failed to get remedial-reading instruction. In the rush to get troops to Vietnam, only about 7.5 percent of them were given such classes.[80]

Aside from lack of funds, there was one big reason why many men failed to be trained in special skills. While standards were lowered to permit them to enter the military, standards were *not* lowered for entry into the hundreds of professional occupations the military offered. Most of the men could not qualify for fields like electronics and bridge building.

Herb DeBose, who served as a first lieutenant in Vietnam, said that many of the Project 100,000 men under his command "did not belong there.... The Army was supposed to teach them a *trade* in something—only they didn't. I had people who could do things only by rote. I found out they could not read. No skills before, no skills after."[81]

While some observers wished that more training had been offered, others felt that training was a waste of time—a hopeless endeavor. "We are being asked to train the untrainable" was the bitter complaint sometimes made by officers and NCOs. Trying to teach skills to low-performing men—often with limited success—took up an inordinate amount of time and resources, forcing instructors to short-change the rest of the troops.

Some Pentagon officials thought that if funds were not available for formal instruction, at least the men could be given on-the-job training. But officers and NCOs complained that some low-aptitude men were unresponsive to hands-on training. An Army supply officer interviewed in 1971 said, "Even in supply, where many of the jobs can be relatively simple, [Project 100,000] men have difficulty. They can't handle the necessary paperwork."[82] Malcolm Riley, a sergeant in an Army transportation unit in 1968, told me that he tried to train two men—both of them "McNamara's Boys" —to drive a military truck. "They wanted to succeed, but they were just too slow in their thinking. So they had to be transferred out."[83]

Specialist 4th Class Terry Hughes of the 553rd Field Combat Support Unit at Fort Hood, Texas, was in charge of a shop that printed labels for uniforms. He told me about one private that he assigned to assemble letters for name tags. "He was supposed to pick out the letters from these little boxes arranged alphabetically. For instance, if we were making a label for SMITH, he would need to get an "S" and then an "M" and so on. This guy took about 30 minutes for each name. He was extremely slow. He didn't know his ABC's in order, and he would hunt around a long time for each letter." Efforts to teach him the correct order of ABC's failed.[84]

While I have focused on Project 100,000 men in the Army and the Marine Corps, I am not forgetting that some of McNamara's Men were assigned to the Air Force and Navy. In those branches, most of the men received little advanced training because they failed to qualify for specialized courses like electronics, communications, and mechanical repair. A former Air Force officer, David Addlestone, remembered Project 100,000 men being used mostly for guard duty. "They'd put them out guarding SAC [Strategic Air Command] bombers in four feet of snow."[85] In the Navy, a former lieutenant recalled, Project 100,000 men lacked "the intelligence to do highly technical and complex duties." Instead they were used to do manual labor such as "lugging around the big, heavy stuff."[86]

For soldiers and Marines who were deemed untrainable for specialized skills, there was one last option—the job of infantry rifleman. "The least capable," said Marine Lieutenant Colonel David Evans, "were sent to do some of the heaviest fighting."[87]

And the result was tragic.

# 22

# The Killing Fields of Vietnam

M ost of the 354,000 men of Project 100,000 went to Vietnam, with about half of them assigned to combat units. A total of 5,478 of these men died while in the service, most of them in combat.[88] Their fatality rate was three times that of other GIs. Although precise figures are unavailable for non-fatal injuries, an estimated 20,270 were wounded, and some were permanently disabled, including an estimated 500 amputees.[89] (All of these tallies would be higher if we knew the number of deaths and injuries of substandard men who were not officially counted in Project 100,000, as will be discussed in Part Five.)

Sending low-IQ men into combat was shocking and shameful. Joseph Galloway, a war correspondent who won a Bronze Star with Valor in Vietnam for carrying wounded men to safety, wrote a column shortly after the death of McNamara entitled "100,000 Reasons to Shed No Tears for McNamara." Project 100,000 men, he said, "were, to put it bluntly, mentally deficient. Illiterate. Mostly black and redneck whites, hailing from the mean big city ghettos and the remote Appalachian valleys. By drafting them the Pentagon would not have to draft an equal number of middle class and elite college boys whose mothers could and would raise hell with their representatives in Washington. The young men of Project 100,000 couldn't read....They had to be taught to tie their boots. They often failed [in basic training], and were recycled over and over until they finally reached some low standard and were declared trained and ready. They could not be taught any more demanding job than trigger-pulling, [so most of them] went straight into combat where the learning curve is steep and deadly. The cold, hard statistics say that these almost helpless young men died in action in the jungles at a rate three times higher than the average draftee....The Good Book says we must forgive those who trespass against us—but what about those who trespass against the most helpless among us; those willing to conscript the mentally handicapped, the most innocent, and turn them into cannon fodder?"[90]

According to Colonel David Hackworth, who fought in both the Korean and Vietnam wars and became one of the most highly decorated warriors in American history, "Project 100,000 was implemented to produce more grunts for the killing fields of Vietnam. It took unfit recruits from the bottom of the barrel and rushed them to Vietnam. The result was human applesauce." He added that for fighting in combat, "ten smart-and-fit soldiers are better than 100 out-of-shape dummies."[91]

One veteran who had a good reason to be dismayed by the deaths of Project 100,000 men in Vietnam was Leslie John Shellhase, who had been wounded in the Battle of the Bulge in World War II and had served as a lieutenant colonel under McNamara at the Pentagon in the 1960's. He said he played a central role in planning Project 100,000, which he considered a bad idea from the start. "We [Pentagon planners] resisted Project 100,000 because we knew that wars are not won by using marginal manpower as cannon fodder, but rather by risking, and sometimes losing, the flower of a nation's youth." He and the other Pentagon planners tried to persuade McNamara to drop Project 100,000. When that effort failed, they proposed altering the program so that military commanders would be barred from sending low-aptitude men into danger zones. "We never envisioned that these men would be used in combat. Instead, we intended for them to be used in service and support areas, where their mental limitations would not cause them to be killed." Unfortunately, Shellhase and his fellow officers failed in their effort to keep Project 100,000 men out of the battlefield.[92]

Lieutenant Paul D. Walker, who served in Vietnam as a platoon leader in the armored cavalry of the 1st Infantry Division, wrote about the worst episode during his tour of duty. "We had not seen a single enemy soldier in two days of combat operations resulting in three killed, ten wounded, and three vehicles destroyed." He blamed the four Project 100,000 men in his platoon who "accounted for more than their share of casualties and accidents." He said that some Project 100,000 men "were virtually untrainable and should never have been allowed into the military, and certainly not sent into combat. Their presence made my job more difficult."[93]

In the later years of the Vietnam War, there was a drop in the effectiveness and morale of the troops. Charles Cooper, a battalion commander in Vietnam, said that by 1970, when he took command, "things were going to hell in a handbasket," and the quality of soldiers had declined. "Thanks to Project 100,000, they were just flooding us with morons and imbeciles. These men couldn't learn well and they'd get frustrated and become aggressive."[94]

In 1971, Congressman William Steiger of Wisconsin made unannounced visits to Fort Meade, Fort Gordon, and Fort Hood to talk to officers and enlisted men about conditions in the Army. "Senior enlisted men complained that the quality of troops had declined significantly and that the growing number of individuals in mental group IV had made training and discipline nearly impossible."[95]

Agreeing that the quality of battlefield troops declined in the last years of the war, William Westmoreland, the commanding general in Vietnam, said that Project 100,000 was a major factor in the decline because it sent "dummies" into the war zone. He estimated that only about 10 percent of the "dummies" could be molded into real soldiers.[96]

Not only were low-quality enlisted men sent to Vietnam, said Westmoreland, but low-quality officers as well. He cited Lieutenant William Calley, convicted in the murder of more than 100 unarmed civilians in the My Lai Massacre in 1968. According to Arnold R. Isaacs, the Vietnam war correspondent for the *Baltimore Sun*, Calley "flunked out of Palm Beach Junior College with two C's, a D, and four F's in his first year and reportedly managed to get through officer candidate school without even learning to read a map or use a compass."[97] Marine Corps Colonel Robert D. Heinl said the Army had to take Calley "because no one else was available."[98] His own attorney used Calley's low intelligence as a courtroom defense: the Army, he said, was to blame for My Lai because if it hadn't lowered mental standards, men like Calley never would have been commissioned. Richard A. Gabriel, who spent 22 years as a U.S. Army officer, says, "Even the staunchest defenders of the Army agree that in normal times a man of Lieutenant Calley's intelligence and predispositions would never have been allowed to hold a commission."[99]

Tony Zinni, a four-star general in the Marine Corps, said, "During Vietnam, the need for bodies had been so great that recruiters were sending people into the military who never should have been there. Promotions came too fast.... People were suddenly wearing grades they were too inexperienced to wear; they did not have the education and training needed to perform complex jobs. Many sergeants weren't real sergeants; and many lieutenants, captains, and even higher should not have held those ranks."[100]

In anecdotes and quotations about Project 100,000, the military often comes off looking bad, so it is worthwhile to emphasize that military leaders didn't want the program. They complained that they were being asked to carry out an impossible task: improving the brain power of men with intellectual disabilities. James Webb, a decorated Marine combat veteran in Vietnam and later a U.S. Senator from Virginia, said that Project 100,000 was designed as a social-science experiment to "test whether mental rejects could function as soldiers. When it was discovered that by and large they could not, the military was blamed for the failure."[101]

But military leaders were blameless. During the early years of the war, when McNamara was campaigning to draft low-aptitude men, wise military commanders and veterans were warning against his misguided idea. For example, in 1964, two years before Project 100,000 was launched, an impassioned article appeared in the *American Bar Association Journal* by a Texas attorney and reserve Air Force Captain, William F. Walsh, who wrote: "Warfare is steadily growing more complex. The day is past when an effective soldier needed only the intelligence to point a musket downhill and obey the order, 'Don't fire till you see the whites of their eyes.' Service in the Armed Forces today requires an alert, questioning mind simply to master the technology of weapons and tactics.... There is likely to be no room for the low-IQ soldier, the 'warm body' who cannot—or will not— 'cut the mustard.' That man... is going to get in the way of those who will have to do the job."[102]

Despite such warnings, McNamara plowed ahead, and the results were disastrous. "One of the single biggest blunders of our Vietnam experience," said Lieutenant Colonel Charles L. Armstrong of the Marine Corps, "was the Project 100,000 folly of taking on board marginally qualified individuals under the mistaken watchword of 'the infantry doesn't have to be real smart.' *Dumb Grunt,* however, is not a complete phrase— *Dumb Dead Grunt* is. You don't have to be a Fulbright Scholar to be a good rifleman (some of the best warriors I know have a fourth grade education), but you can't be stupid."[103]

To survive in combat, you had to be smart. You had to know how to use your rifle effectively and keep it clean and operable, how to navigate through jungles and rice paddies without alerting the enemy, and how to communicate and cooperate with other members of your team.

Sad to say, many low-aptitude men were not smart enough to be successful in combat, and as a result, they were killed or wounded.

# 23

# Casualties of War

Barry Romo and his nephew Robert ended up in Vietnam at the same time. (Barry explained that he had a brother named Harold who was 27 years older than he was, and Harold had a son named Robert.) "I loved Robert like a brother. We grew up together. He was only one month younger."

Barry served in Vietnam as an infantry platoon leader in 1967-68, and he saw a lot of combat, winning a Bronze Star for his courage on the battlefield. During his tour, he learned that Robert had been drafted and was being trained at Fort Lewis, Washington, to be an infantryman, destined for Vietnam. Barry was alarmed because Robert was "very slow" and had failed the Army's mental test. But then along came Project 100,000, lowering standards and making him draftable. A host of people—his relatives, his comrades at Fort Lewis, his sergeants and officers—wrote to the commanding general at Fort Lewis, asking that Robert not be sent into combat because, as one relative put it, "he would die." But the general turned down the request.

Once in Vietnam, Robert was sent to an infantry unit near the border of North Vietnam, one of the most dangerous combat areas. During a patrol, he was shot in the neck while trying to help a wounded friend. He did not die instantly, but heavy gunfire kept a medic from reaching him. "He drowned in his own blood," said Barry.

At the request of the family, Barry was given permission to leave Vietnam and accompany Robert's body home to Rialto,

California. The aluminum coffin was sealed and draped with a flag, and the family was not allowed to view the remains. (It was Army policy to discourage or forbid viewing when a body was badly mutilated.)

Looking back, Barry said that Robert "really didn't have much luck. While others were getting deferments, he was drafted. While Congressmen's sons were getting 4-F's [exemptions] for braces on their teeth, Robert was drafted as part of Project 100,000."

In a speech delivered 42 years later, Barry Romo said that the family had never recovered from losing Robert. "His death almost destroyed us with anger and sorrow."[104]


Mental slowness and extreme anxiety were among the worst enemies of Project 100,000 men in combat. "While training at Fort Benning," says Lieutenant Colonel Robert Kimball, a combat veteran of the Vietnam war, "we had the idea cemented into our heads that there were two kinds of soldiers: the quick and the dead." To survive in combat, you had to be quick to recognize a threat and quick to respond to it. All soldiers in combat experience fear, and "fear causes a soldier to slow down," he said. "Fear can have a major impact on whether or not a soldier survives war."[105]

If fear can slow down the thinking of an ordinary soldier, imagine what it does for a soldier who is slow-witted to begin with. Sergeant Major Francis T. McNeive, who served with the Marine Corps in Vietnam in 1966-67 and again in 1969-70, said that "people who were borderline retarded did not respond fast enough... and that's how people became casualties."[106]

Describing soldiers in the 60th Infantry who fought in a battle for Saigon in May, 1968, military historian Keith William Nolan writes that Lieutenant Frank Neild had a radioman, PFC James Hewitt (not his real name), who was "big, dumb, and nice—a nineteen-year-old piece of cannon fodder from rural Pennsylvania. He was nicknamed Lurch because of his glazed expression and half-opened mouth." His superiors "found it hard to believe that anyone as slow as Hewitt could have passed the aptitude tests required for military service, and chalked him up as one of McNamara's 100,000, the infamous program by which the services were forced to accept a hundred-thousand substandard recruits per year, the better to protect the sons of the upper class from Vietnam."[107]

Hewitt "wanted desperately to do a good job as the team radioman, but could not figure out how to adjust frequencies." Lieutenant Neild "tried to coach him, but nothing stuck," and the lieutenant finally asked his superior to replace Hewitt "with a trooper who actually knew how to operate a radio." Neild said that Hewitt's "character was impeccable. His only problem was that he couldn't think." While waiting to be replaced, Hewitt was grievously wounded in combat, and he died two weeks later.

Marine Captain David Anthony Dawson said, "Men who could not understand simple orders or perform simple tasks clearly posed a danger to themselves and the other members of their unit." He gave the following example: "While serving as a battalion commander in Vietnam, Brigadier General William Weise watched a squad leader give an order for an ambush patrol. The squad leader gave a simple, clear order, but one Marine couldn't remember any of the crucial details, including the password. That night, this Marine left the ambush to relieve himself without telling anyone. When returning, he wandered into the kill zone. The squad leader sprang the ambush and his squad killed him."[108]

"The dull-witted soldier," said Pentagon official Eliot Cohen, "does not simply get himself killed—he causes the death of others as well."[109] According to Chief Warrant Officer

4 William S. Tuttle, a Vietnam veteran, "If you take someone with an IQ of 40 and give him a rifle, he's more dangerous to you than he is to the enemy. I almost got shot twice and had one guy almost nail me with a LAW [light anti-armor weapon] when he was startled by a sudden noise. If you put [a low-IQ man] in an infantry patrol, you have to spend most of your time making sure he doesn't kill a friendly [a comrade] by accident, and doesn't get himself killed during contact because he's totally unaware of what's going on around him. Imagine sending a five-year-old into combat. That's what Project 100,000 was all about."[110]

G.J. Lau, an Army veteran who served with the 1st Infantry Division in 1969, remembered Jerry (not his real name), who was a member of "McNamara's 100,000"—guys who "were not exactly your best or your brightest." One night "Jerry was out on the Quan Loi Green Line [perimeter] standing night guard. A very popular officer had been out setting his men in position and was returning to inside the wire. There is a challenge procedure, just like you see in the movies. 'Halt, who goes there?' 'Lt. So-and-So.' 'Advance and be recognized.' That's not it exactly, but you get the idea. You order the person to halt and then do whatever it takes to identify them as friend or foe, normally not a difficult task given the obvious differences between the average NVA or VC and us."

But for some reason, "Jerry saw the officer approaching and shouted out 'Halt,' and then immediately opened fire, killing him on the spot."

The killing caused consternation in the camp. "The men under the officer's command immediately made it known to any and all that Jerry was a dead man. Period. End of discussion. Someone must have taken that threat pretty seriously, because Jerry was gone at first light. Never saw him again."[111]

New, inexperienced men in Army and Marine units—especially Project 100,000 men—had a high rate of getting themselves and their comrades wounded or killed in the first few months of their tours in Vietnam. James R. Ebert found that 43 percent of Army fatalities happened in the first three months. He quotes the recollections of an Army infantryman named Michael Jackson about a squad on patrol: "This real goofy dude who hadn't been in country very long didn't have his M-16 safety on. They were coming up a little knoll that was real steep and muddy, and this guy's M-16 discharged accidentally and shot another guy in the foot. The M-16 round tumbles. It isn't a clean round, it is a messy round. It went in his foot and came out in his leg and he died of shock. He had something like two weeks to go [before leaving Vietnam]."[112]

One veteran said that new guys "talked too loud and made too much noise while moving around, didn't know what to take into the bush or even how to wear it properly, couldn't respond to basic combat commands, fired too much ammo, and tended to flake out on even the easiest 10-klick [kilometer] moves."[113]

Robert Nylen, a combat infantry officer with the First Air Cavalry Division, remembered a new man, Finder (not his real name), who arrived via helicopter. "Descending, Finder looked at his new mates with dull, fearful eyes. It didn't take X-ray vision to tell he was a dud, a loser. Finder would endanger himself and his colleagues from the moment he hopped off the chopper. It wasn't his fault. He was a sad-sack member of Robert McNamara's Nearly-Special-Needs Army. Defense Secretary McNamara had lowered recruiting standards to permit borderline dopes into the service. In the late Sixties, recruits were in demand, even dimwitted ones."

Sure enough, only one month later, because he was clumsy and careless and not alert while on patrol, Finder overlooked a rusted trip wire and triggered a Chi-Com [Chinese Communist] grenade. The booby trap ripped off his right ear and drove shrapnel into his shoulder and forearm. The man behind him was hit by shards that lacerated an arm, a shoulder, and his right hand. Both men were medevaced to a hospital.

Before Finder's encounter with a booby trap, said Nylen, "we knew him as a guy who'd joined to get his brown teeth fixed. Military service was often a poor kid's first opportunity to see a dentist. Now Finder's face is no longer connected to his left ear. A chunk of his shoulder is gone, too."[114]

Mines and booby traps were a major cause of deaths and injuries in Vietnam, especially for new guys. Bill Peters, who served with the First Force Recon Company of the Marine Corps in 1969, received a package from his mother containing a recent *Life* magazine that featured a section called "Those Who Died in Vietnam This Week." He was stunned to see the names and photos of three of his Marine buddies with whom he had flown into Vietnam. "The thing that had the greatest impact on me was the fact that my friends had all died within their first month in Vietnam, and their deaths were not attributed to direct enemy contact but to mines and booby traps."[115] Of the 5,478 Project 100,000 men who died in the service, an estimated 1,300 were killed by mines and booby traps.[116]

## 24

# "Rich Man's War and a Poor Man's Fight"

John L. Ward rejoiced when Project 100,000 came into his life.

He grew up in poverty in a black neighborhood of Glasgow, Missouri, living in a shanty that had no running water. "When I was in high school, black people still could not sit in a white-owned restaurant and drink a soda or eat a hamburger. They had to go to the back door, the side alley, or some other place designated 'for colored only.'"

Ward dreamed of escaping Glasgow by joining the military when he got out of high school. But his hopes were dashed when he scored too low on the military's entrance test. With the military option closed to him, he started planning to move to a big city like Kansas City or Des Moines.

"Then, to my utter surprise, the Marine Corps recruiter showed up, and explained to me that I could join them now"—despite the low test score. Thanks to Project 100,000 and the newly lowered standards, "I could now pursue my dream of getting out of Glasgow and seeing the world."

His presence in Project 100,000 meant that he had scored in Category IV on the mental test, but his later accomplishments revealed that he was not a man with intellectual disabilities. (He probably scored in the higher level of Category IV, as described in Chapter 19). He possessed sound native intelligence and a desire to succeed—the characteristics that McNamara assumed (erroneously) would be shared by *all* Project 100,000 men.

Ward became a proud Marine and he quickly won a promotion to corporal, but unfortunately his dreams were shattered in Vietnam. During the night of August 18, 1968, enemy troops attacked and overran Marine bunkers at Phu Loc, killing 17 Marines and wounding many more. Ward suffered severe injuries, and he was returned to the United States for a long and painful recovery. His disabilities included:

o   Chronic encephalopathy (brain damage) with manifestations of cluster migraine headaches, dizziness, ocular imbalance, and loss of memory
o   Post-Traumatic Stress Disorder (PTSD)
o   Depression
o   Wounds to right leg
o   Amputation of right ring finger, right pinkie finger, and the ankylosed joint of middle finger
o   Loss of use of right hand
o   Ruptured eardrums (both ears)
o   Brain concussion
o   Compound skull fracture
o   Hemorrhaging of optic nerves (both eyes)
o   Transplantation of lenses in both eyes
o   Ongoing inflammation in both eyes, causing further deterioration of vision
o   Irritable bowel syndrome
o   Immunodeficiency
o   Skin rashes/lesions
o   Thyroid dysfunction
o   Side-effects from steroids
o   Colon spasms
o   Multiple tumors and sarcoidosis
o   Sarcoid rheumatoid arthritis

After leaving the service (with the rank of sergeant), Ward spent 15 years just trying to survive his physical and mental torments. Eventually he became a counselor and advocate for Project 100,000 veterans. In 2012, he wrote a book entitled *Moron Corps* about his experiences as one of McNamara's "morons"—a term that he hated but nevertheless embraced to remind America that Project 100,000 was "insensitive, morally unjust, and inhumane." He said that the men who were accepted under McNamara's program served their country honorably. "Even with our so-called limited abilities, we were willing to lay down our lives for our country." But the program was carried out in a "morally shameful" manner. Project 100,000 men were overrepresented in combat, and they "died in disproportionate numbers." Those who managed to survive were "thrown back into society without the skills promised us." Many of the men were homeless and suffered from "isolation, unemployment, drug addiction, and medical neglect." Many failed to receive the assistance that they were supposed to receive from the U.S. Department of Veterans Affairs.

Helping McNamara's victims and fighting for their rights "was the battle I became caught up in, and consumed by. This was a battle I fought over and over again, continuing long after the Vietnam War was over."[117]

Ward and many other men on the lower rungs of the economic ladder went to Vietnam to make up for the absence of men on the upper rungs. In an earlier chapter, I pointed out that actor George Hamilton won a hardship deferment because he was the sole support of his mother, who lived in his Hollywood mansion. "Hamilton's case," wrote author Natalie M. Rosinsky, "contrasted with the experience of many black draftees in the southern United States. In the South, mostly all-white draft boards often discriminated against blacks." She cited the case of Edward Neal, a black youth in Mississippi who "had two jobs and was the sole support of his mother, disabled father, and eight brothers and sisters. He went to his draft board to request a hardship deferment but was denied." He ended up in Vietnam.[118]

Because the National Guard and Reserves were relatively safe avenues for military service, they were filled to capacity with middle-class and wealthy men, mostly white. You usually had to have connections to get in. Poor and working class men, especially blacks, were virtually excluded. In 1968, the Army National Guard was only 1.26 percent black. In Mississippi, where blacks made up 42 percent of the population, only one black man was admitted to the 10,365-man Mississippi National Guard.[119]

Robert McNamara may have been sincere in wanting to lift underprivileged men out of poverty, but was it fair to ask the poor to bear a disproportionate burden of combat? Toward the end of the war, in 1972, Professor Leslie Fiedler, who knew hundreds of young people at his college (State University of New York at Buffalo), slowly realized that he knew not a single Vietnam veteran. "And I had never known a single family that had lost a son in Vietnam." The reason, he concluded, was that Vietnam was the first war that "has been fought for us by our servants... the actual fighting of the war has become more and more exclusively an occupation of the exploited and dispossessed."[120]

In world history, such unfairness was nothing new. Plutarch, a historian in ancient Greece, noted that in his day, impoverished soldiers "fight and die to protect the rich and luxurious lifestyle enjoyed by others."[121] In the American Civil War, wealthy men dodged the draft by taking advantage of a law that permitted them to pay someone else to fight in their place. For example, billionaire Andrew Carnegie paid an Irish immigrant $850 to take his place in the ranks. (That amount would be $17,300 in today's dollars.) Under the rallying cry of "Rich Man's War and a Poor Man's Fight," anti-draft riots broke out in Northern cities. In a riot in New York City in 1863, an estimated 120 people were killed and over 200 injured.[122] During the Vietnam War, Congressman William A. Steiger of Wisconsin said, "The draft survives as a last vestige of the ancient custom whereby the rich and powerful forced the poor and weak to provide service at subsistence wages."[123]

While it was true that men who had grown up in poverty were disproportionately represented in combat, I don't want to leave the impression that only the extremely poor fought in Vietnam. In infantry units, the poor were joined by many men from working-class families—described by historian Christian G. Appy as "the nineteen-year-old children of waitresses, factory workers, truck drivers, secretaries, firefighters, carpenters, custodians, police officers, salespeople, clerks, mechanics, miners, and farmworkers."[124] Men from lower economic levels (poor and working class) comprised 80 percent of combat forces, while the remaining 20 percent came from the middle class, half of them serving as officers.

One of the ugliest aspects of the Vietnam era was the disdain that some smart and wealthy Americans felt toward the unfortunates who were sent into combat in Vietnam. In 1967, one student who was privileged to sit out the war in college told an interviewer that Vietnam was "for the dummies, the losers."[125] A 1971 Harris survey found that most Americans believed that those who went to Vietnam were "suckers."[126] William Broyles, who commanded a Marine infantry platoon in Vietnam in 1969-1971, said, "It was not a privilege to be able to fight; it was instead evidence that one had failed to understand how to manipulate the system, as if anyone not smart enough to get a deferment or at least to get a job in the rear was too dumb to do anything but carry a rifle."[127]

# 25

# Walking Point

In August, 1968, at an encampment called Fire Base Nancy, one low-IQ soldier played a deadly joke, according to Robert Nylen, the infantry platoon leader previously quoted. "For several days, a private in Robert McNamara's 'breathe-and-you're-in' Army had played the same grotesque joke." He pulled the pin on a hand grenade and then rolled the grenade toward his mates. "The first time he pulled this depraved stunt, his mates scattered, terrified. Nothing happened." The man laughed, explaining that he had disabled the grenade (by pulling out the detonator cylinder), and "his goggle-eyed mates pummeled him: 'Never again, Bozo!' He played the same trick the next day; this time, his mates beat him harder. The third day he pulled his idiotic stunt, his mates flinched, sighed, muttered, and kept eating. They wouldn't fall for the lame gag again." But this time, the man had forgotten to disable the grenade. It exploded, killing two soldiers and wounding several others. As punishment, Nylen recommended that the man *not* be sent to the States to be tried for manslaughter because he would probably spend ten years in a prison watching TV. Instead, a worse fate was to keep him in Vietnam and make him perform risky duties such as walking point.[128]

Walking point was one of the most dangerous assignments in Vietnam because you walked at the front of your squad or platoon in a combat operation. You risked tripping a booby trap, detonating a landmine, or walking into an ambush. Also you were "sniper bait," the easiest man for an enemy soldier to pick off. Many units assigned the task to seasoned veterans because the point man needed to have savvy and a cool head—his alertness could save lives.[129] In some units, however, FNGs (fuckin' new guys), also known as cherries, were chosen, and sometimes Vietnamese civilians were forced at gunpoint to walk point to detonate landmines and booby traps.[130] Over the years, I heard stories of low-IQ soldiers being assigned to walk point. For example, Wayne Johnson, who served as a "grunt" [infantryman] in Vietnam in 1968, told me that his squad leader assigned one of "McNamara's Boys" to walk point, and justified his action by saying "if anybody has to die, better a dummy than the rest of us." Johnson said, "It was unfair, I know, but none of us protested." While he was with the unit, he added, none of the point men were injured or killed.[131]

By contrast, some commanders tried to keep low-IQ men out of danger. Military historian Keith William Nolan wrote that in the 31st Infantry's combat operations in Saigon in May, 1968, Sergeant Kenneth Davis reported that he had several unreliable soldiers in his squad, including "blank-eyed members of McNamara's 100,000. Davis used these unreliable men as pack mules to carry extra ammunition and extra weapons. 'If you can't do anything else,' Davis instructed these duds, 'just bring the weapons and ammo up to me and the team leaders when we need 'em.'"[132]

In an infantry platoon in 1968, Lieutenant Gary B. Roberts commanded three Project 100,000 men who had "substandard intelligence," but had been given rifles and placed in a maneuver battalion out in the jungle. "They were just stupid," he said. Sending them to a combat unit was a criminal act on the part of the Army. He said he blocked them from going into combat. "I just kept them with me [in platoon headquarters] to watch them to make sure they didn't hurt themselves, hurt anybody else, or have somebody else shoot them just to get rid of them."[133]

Regarding this last remark, I occasionally heard rumors of low-IQ men being deliberately killed to enhance the safety of fellow soldiers, but I could not verify a single case. Gerry Barker, a sergeant with the 1st Cavalry Division, said, "I heard stories of platoon sergeants who shot one of their privates" because the ineptitude of one man could cause not only his death but also the deaths of other men. Barker provided no specifics.[134]

William Broyles, the previously mentioned Marine lieutenant, told of one young Marine named March who "was profoundly dense...he kept falling asleep at the worst times— on watch or on an ambush. I woke him up once by holding an M-16 next to his head and letting off a magazine on full automatic. It did no good. On one ambush he dozed off, rolled over in his sleep, and fell into the river. On another ambush he was gently awakened by the sound of his comrades firing at three NVA [North Vietnamese] soldiers who had been standing above him with their AK-47s pointed at his head. Such behavior put the whole platoon in jeopardy; in combat everyone is totally dependent on everyone else. March was in imminent danger of being conveniently shot during our next contact with the enemy, so I sent him back to the rear to do some punishment work."[135]

Dan Evans, a combat medic who served with the 4/39th infantry unit of the 9th Infantry Division, told of a soldier named Browner, who was "worthless, like many of McNamara's 100,000 boys" and utterly unable to handle the stress of jungle warfare. During one mission, he was supposed to carry the medic's bag, but he ran away, leaving the medic without extra supplies for treating the wounded during an ensuing firefight. On another occasion, while sitting and waiting during an attempted ambush, he shot himself in the foot "in the hope of getting shipped home." His foot healed, but his platoon mates didn't want him to go into the field with them because his unreliable, erratic behavior endangered the lives of everyone in the platoon. "Someone voiced the common opinion that maybe some gook sniper would do us the favor of pinging his ferrety ass," said Evans. Thereafter, Browner was kept as a platoon member but was not allowed to go out on patrols.[136]

George Buford, the veteran cited earlier, tells of an intelligent infantryman who survived Vietnam by actually volunteering to walk point whenever his platoon was on patrol—not because he was heroic, but because he feared that some of his low-IQ platoon mates might lead the unit into an ambush. "Dangerous as walking point was—and it was very dangerous—he felt that he was still safer doing it himself rather than trusting anyone else to do it."[137]

# 26

# Stories Told by Veterans

Here is a mélange of recollections by Army, Marine Corps, and Air Force veterans:

Gregory D. Foster, a West Point graduate who commanded an infantry company of the Americal Division in Vietnam, tells of a reunion of his infantry buddies. "We laughed when we recalled the doofus GI in our company who shot himself in the foot in the hope of getting evacuated from the field. We couldn't agree on whether he was actually smart enough to do such a thing intentionally. Characteristically, though, he failed—the bullet passed between two of his toes and took off just enough skin to make walking painful."[138]

Lewis B. Puller Jr., a Marine platoon leader who lost both legs and one hand in a booby trap explosion in 1968, said that his machine-gun team "had a forty-year-old man who was completely bald and it seemed to me somewhat mentally deficient. His nickname was Pappy... and he had entered the Marine Corps through an ill-conceived program called Project 100,000, which was designed to give hard-core unemployed civilians a skill that they could use after their military service.... I had a hard time figuring out how his skills with a machine gun were going to help him earn a living after the Marine Corps."[139]

Dr. Lawrence William, who was an Army doctor in Vietnam (1968-1969), wrote, "The men of McNamara's 100,000 had more than their share of medical problems. I remember one particular example of the unfortunates who came to see me on sick call. He said that it burned when he peed. But, unlike most with this problem, he denied having any penile drip. So, I asked him to give me a urine sample in one of my small, sterile, lidded plastic cups. "No, sir," he replied, "I can't do that, sir!' "Well," I said, "Just take this canteen of water, drink the whole thing and wait around until the urge takes you, and then put a urine sample in this cup." He protested several additional times but I gave him the canteen and sent him over to the other side of the Quonset hut while I saw 6 or 7 other soldiers that morning. I had forgotten about him and his problem until he returned to me about an hour later and handed me the cup with about 15 cc of viscid fluid in it. Under my microscope, it was obvious that this was a semen sample! It turned out he did not know what urine was at all!"[140]

Dr. William also tells a sad story. While in Vietnam, he received a letter from a congressman who wanted a certain infantryman to be examined because his mother claimed, "My son is suffering from black syphilis of the stomach and no one helps him." Dr. William had the soldier flown to his clinic for a medical examination, but found "no medical problems of any sort, other than his mental retardation"—he had the mind of a child. Dr. William sent the man back to his unit in the field. But two months later the mother again complained that her son was not receiving proper medical treatment, so "the whole process was restarted and I was again directed to respond to a congressional inquiry about the man. The fellow was relocated and I had him flown back to the barracks in Dong Tam for me to examine again. Once more I carefully examined him and again found that he was not ill in any way. He went back to the barracks after my examination. That night Dong Tam was mortared. This man with a child's mind was in his bed sleeping when an incoming round hit his barracks building and killed him. He was the only fatality. Unfortunately, this soldier was one of the troops referred to as McNamara's Morons."[141]

Although the Air Force received relatively few Project 100,000 men, their presence was noted. H. Michael Sweeney, a jet engine mechanic for the Air Force's Strategic Air Command, remembered an airman who "was not known for being terribly bright. A big, lumbering oaf of a guy, he was slow as molasses both in body and in mind. Someone once bet him one dollar he could not eat one dozen doughnuts in one minute. He won that bet, but when he was done, his mouth was bleeding from the attempt."[142]

During the Vietnam War, according to former drill instructor Gregg Stoner, every platoon in Marine boot camp ended up with at least one "Gomer Pyle," named after the goofy private in the 1960s TV sitcom *Gomer Pyle USMC*. Each Gomer, said Stoner, was an unteachable "idiot" who was always performing drill movements incorrectly. So, whenever there was an inspection or a contest, drill instructors made sure that Gomer was sent to sick bay so that he was unavailable to march in front of visiting officers.

Stoner told of one incident that seemed straight out of a TV episode of *Gomer Pyle*, but actually happened while he was checking recruits' two pairs of boots for correct fit by having them stand on a footlocker, which was placed outdoors. "One recruit I was inspecting appeared on my footlocker wearing two *right* boots. I couldn't believe it! I yelled at the private: 'You idiot! What in hell are you doing wearing two right boots?' He replied 'Sir, there must have been a mix up and the private was issued two right boots, sir!' I immediately got right into his face and screamed: 'Private—get your dumb ass back inside and get the other boots and get back here right away. Do you understand me?' 'Sir, yes sir!' and off he went to the Quonset hut. Moments later he was back. He jumped up on the footlocker, this time wearing two *left* boots. In a very exasperated voice he said: 'Sir, the private's other two boots were two left boots, sir!'"[143]

Speaking of Marines, weren't they supposed to be an elite branch with nothing but eager volunteers? Yes, the Marine Corps traditionally filled its ranks with 100% volunteers, but during the Vietnam War, it was required to accept draftees. Dr. Ronald Glasser, an Army physician said, "I was drafted in the summer of 1968. The [military] was running out of everything, including doctors and Marines. At the induction center, I saw the draftees lined up and there was a Marine sergeant walking down the line saying, 'One, two, three, Marine.' It wasn't necessarily a death sentence, but it was probably not where they wanted to be going. Marines were being killed in Vietnam then platoon by platoon."[144]

Joel S. Franks remembered that in his basic training squad in 1969, there was a soldier who "was so exceedingly dimwitted that he had to be reminded to shower and change his clothes."[145]

"Every platoon has a fool," according to writer Jack Todd, who went through Army basic training at Fort Lewis in 1969. "Ours is a bigger fool than most. His name is Fillmore, he comes from Idaho, he has a sloping forehead and buck teeth, and he does not belong in the Army.... On the rifle range, we do everything for him: load his clips with bullets, twenty to a clip, load the clips in the rifle, show him how to point, aim, and squeeze." Despite all the help, Fillmore screws up and almost shoots Todd and a sergeant by accident. One night, Fillmore "comes in and walks right across the carefully waxed and buffed floor in the center of the barracks, the place you are never, ever supposed to walk except in your socks, leaving great, muddy tracks from his combat boots. I shout at him to move or take off his boots. Pretty soon the whole platoon is yelling at Fillmore to get his dumb ass out of the middle of the floor and to take off his fucking muddy combat boots. Fillmore stares at us, blinks a couple of time like he did on the rifle range, and keeps walking, leaving a thick, muddy track with every step."[146]

A former Army officer who identified himself as FJB on a veterans' Internet forum, said that in 1967, he was the commander of a company at Fort Belvoir, Virginia. He related the story of a Private Caputo from New Jersey, who was drafted—despite being diagnosed as "cognitively deficient"—under the new standards of Robert McNamara ("who deserves to burn in hell" because of Project 100,000). At one point, 560 soldiers in his company were given a weekend pass. "Under the rules," he said, "all 560 of them had to sign out of the morning book, an official Army document. Almost 600 men signing out on a single document takes time, so First Sergeant Hatley was pushing the kids through as fast as possible. The procedure was: On a single line of the book, the soldier prints his full name, signs it, prints his destination and the date and time. Things went smoothly, in Army assembly-line fashion, until Private Caputo's turn. Then, he screwed it up not once, not twice, but four times. I could see from Hatley's expression that he was about ready to shoot Caputo, but he mastered himself. Pulling Caputo from the line and positioning him next to himself, the First Sergeant called PFC Carpenter, the next man, forward and told him to sign out. Then he turned to Caputo and said loudly and forcefully, 'Look at what he does and do the same fucking thing! Exactly the same thing!' And so Caputo did. Exactly the same thing. He printed the name 'Leotis Carpenter,' signed it, neatly added Carpenter's destination—Jackson, Tennessee— and stood there beaming proudly. Sergeant Hatley was never the same man afterward."[147]

One veteran recalled a man in boot camp "who didn't know his right from left and other simple commands while in formation or marching. He was always pissing off the drill instructor. When you talked to this troop, he had this vacant look in his eyes. He couldn't read or talk very well. If I had to guess, his IQ was maybe 50-60. He made it through boot camp. It was sad to see the military drafting someone like this, then putting a weapon in his hands and sending him to Vietnam to be killed or get somebody else killed. I know if I was on patrol and had him in my unit, I would be very concerned. The only reason I wasn't sent into the bush was because I am color blind. I couldn't distinguish a tree from a gook at 50 yards. It is strange how they saw my eyes as a handicap, and yet they saw someone who was low-IQ and illiterate as not handicapped."[148]

Sergeant James Ferguson recalled that soon after arriving in Vietnam, his air cavalry squadron was flown out of home base in helicopters to search a small Vietnamese village. "We searched the village and set up later in a perimeter to wait for the extraction choppers. As we waited for the extraction, Private Sam Judd [not his real name] fell asleep and no one on his assigned ship or our ground control realized that he didn't get on the chopper. When we got back to home base, his platoon realized he was missing and we were sent back out to locate him. We went back to the pickup point and started searching back to the village. Judd was in the center of the village sitting with the *mama-sans* [older Vietnamese women] drinking Coke, his favorite beverage. He was sitting there like a little kid with no worries on his mind. He just laughed about being left behind because he fell asleep. To understand how Private Judd could have been left behind with all the chopper noise and everyone moving around him, you must have a little more information. Judd had a low IQ and really had no understanding of the Army, war or really about life in general. In my opinion he had been sent through Basic and AIT by a bunch of people who just wanted to pass him on to someone else to straighten him out. They had no time for the paperwork that would be required to get him a Section 8 [a discharge for being mentally unfit]. I see Judd every time I watch *Full Metal Jacket*, but not as someone dangerous, just some child who has no idea what is happening around him. Everyone in our outfit tried to look out for him, but this one time we all fell short. A few days after that, he was just gone from the unit with no explanations." Ferguson was never able to find out what happened to Judd.[149]

McNamara's 100,000 program "was a disaster for those who actually had to serve with and supervise these soldiers," said Lieutenant Colonel John Gross, in recalling his time as a company commander in the 9th Infantry Division in Vietnam. For example, "we were assigned a cook who appeared to have Down syndrome. We were so worried about him, the first sergeant told the mess sergeant to assign someone to keep an eye on him at all times. We thought he might wander off somewhere."

As another example of men who never should have been accepted into the Army, Gross related a story about Sergeant Harkins (not his real name), a "totally incompetent" man who had been promoted to the rank of sergeant for reasons that were "a mystery to me." (At the time of this incident, some low-ranking enlisted men were rapidly promoted to sergeant because their platoons had been decimated in combat, and replacement sergeants were urgently needed.)

"One morning," said Gross, "as an ambush patrol came in, one of the soldiers approached me."

"Sergeant Harkins was our patrol leader last night," said the soldier. "Sir, he went out without a bolt in his weapon and he had no idea of what he was supposed to do."

"What?" Gross said.

"It's true, Sir. Yesterday, when he said he couldn't find his bolt, I helped him look for it. I think when he cleaned his weapon in an ammo can full of gasoline, he threw out the bolt when he emptied the gas. He didn't seem worried. He said no one would know the difference."

"When I confronted Harkins about the bolt-less weapon," Gross said, "he looked at me with a totally vacant expression.

Speaking with an impediment, he simply said, without any hint of regret, remorse or concern, 'I wost my bowt.'"

He was immediately moved to a rear area.[150]

# 27

# Walking Wounded

To justify lowering test scores for entry into the military, Robert McNamara said that Project 100,000 men "were not brain-poor at birth, but only privilege-poor, advantage-poor, opportunity-poor."[151] His description was accurate, but only when applied to those men in Category IV who possessed "street smarts"—a sound native intelligence. They did poorly on the AFQT not because of mental deficiency but because of substandard education, learning disabilities, or weak testing skills. Some of them were successful in the military, as I will show later in this book.

What McNamara failed to see was that many Project 100,000 were incurably limited. They were indeed "brain-poor" for life, with no hope of making huge mental improvements. No amount of McNamara's audiovisual gadgetry could transform them from slow learners into bright, or even average, citizens.

But wait a minute: hadn't psychologists discovered that even people with serious mental limitations were capable of absorbing much more training than society had previously thought possible? Yes, and it was a valuable insight: mentally limited persons were not hopeless—they were capable of growth and maturity. But here was the problem: they might be able to learn how to make change, but that didn't mean that they could someday create a spreadsheet. They might be able to learn how to put together parts in a factory assembly line, but that didn't mean they could someday operate a 105mm howitzer in battle. There was no hope of dramatically lifting the IQ of Project

100,000 men who missed a test question like this: "If a farmer had a bucket of 24 eggs and he stumbled and broke half of them, how many eggs would he have left?"

The men who missed such questions were slow learners who were able to live happy, productive lives if they had a protective environment—a cozy haven with loving parents, helpful friends, and sympathetic bosses. Such was not the case for many Project 100,000 men. With its bellowing sergeants, rowdy soldiers, and extreme stress, the Army was as far from a cozy haven as slow learners could find. In his book *Military Men*, Ward Just described dull-witted soldiers at Fort Lewis: "Those with IQs of eighty, the ones called Shitkick and Fuckhead, the clumsy ones who arrive at Lewis and are instantly diverted into remedial reading drills.... These men proceed through the Army as they proceed through life: walking wounded in the center of a monstrous joke."[152]

*Walking wounded.* An apt description of the mentally limited men who served in the Armed Forces. Throughout their service time, many of these men were ridiculed for their ignorance and clumsiness. They were called names like dumbass, lamebrain, dimwit, idiot, dolt, and knucklehead. They were cheated out of their money and tricked into taking KP for other men. They were the victims of pranks such as shaving cream being foamed into their boots while they slept, the deed usually done shortly before awakening so that the foam was still puffy and looked like whipped cream.

Over the years, American military leaders agreed that low-IQ men took longer to train than the average soldier, and they performed poorly. Anxiety and stress overwhelmed them, and they had a hard time thinking quickly and clearly. Therefore these men should not be conscripted unless there was a serious shortage of manpower. And if they had to be drafted, they should be used only for menial tasks performed away from the battlefield. They certainly must never to be used in combat.

The universal wisdom of field commanders was: fight with the most competent warriors you can find.

Rejecting this wisdom and replacing it with psychological theories and sociological panaceas of the 1960s, McNamara let low-ability men be assigned to combat. He did this not because he was a heartless warlord bent upon using "marginal" men as worthless throwaways, but because, in his optimism and naiveté, he failed to recognize that many low-aptitude men were indeed "brain-poor," incapable of ever becoming competent, efficient soldiers.[153] It was a misjudgment that would have grievous results.

David Addleston, an attorney who championed veterans' rights, said that Project 100,000 men and their families before, during, and after the war were hampered by one troublesome fact: "They were the last to write letters." In other words, they didn't know how to communicate effectively—how to stand up for their rights, and how to overcome obstacles.[154]

Earlier, I showed how tens of thousands of middle-class and upper-class men beat the draft by employing such strategies as getting the family doctor to write a letter attesting to some minor medical problem. By contrast, most low-income youths knew nothing about how they could manage their draft status. In many cases, they had legitimate problems that should have kept them from serving—such as being blind in one eye or having only one kidney—but they possessed no awareness or skills to argue their case.[155] They didn't know that they could go to a draft board or induction center and explain their rightful grounds for an exemption. Later, if they were abused in basic training or AIT, they lacked the skills to complain to a member of Congress. After discharge, if they were denied veterans' benefits, they didn't know how to work through the bureaucracy.

In my research, I found only one case of a Project 100,000 man or his family using the tools of protest and persuasion that middle-class citizens knew how to use. In 1969, a father in Oregon fought the Army's plan to send his son—whom he described as "retarded with the mental age of a 10-year-old"—to Vietnam as an infantryman. His mother said, "He's just a little boy. He'd be killed sure." The parents generated publicity in Oregon newspapers and enlisted the aid of Congressman Wendell Wyatt and Senator Mark Hatfield. Because of all the negative publicity, the Army cancelled the youth's assignment to combat in Vietnam and sent him instead to Germany to perform clerical tasks.[156]

Imagine how different Project 100,000 would have turned out if thousands of families had been capable of raising a hue and cry over their mentally subnormal sons being sent into combat. Many lives would have been saved.

# 28

# Going Crazy

During my lifetime, in moments of extreme stress, anxiety, or panic, I have done things that are dumb and destructive. It is humbling and instructive to remember my own episodes of dysfunction when I consider the insane actions of some Project 100,000 men, who were young (typically 19 or 20) and burdened with more anxiety and vulnerability than I will ever experience.

Dr. Douglas Bey, a combat psychiatrist for the 1st Infantry Division in Vietnam, tells the story of a Project 100,000 man, PFC White (not his real name), who was "charged with destruction of government property and attempted murder after blowing up a mess hall that was fortunately empty." Following his arrest he was described as "a pudgy, disheveled, dull-eyed Caucasian, with streaks of tears on his face and a runny nose. The lack of sparkle in his eyes and his tendency to breathe through his mouth gave him the appearance of being dull."

Before his violent outburst, his first sergeant had protected him "from being picked on" by other men. The sergeant "saw him as a good kid who was not very bright." But one day the sergeant, for some reason, was away from the camp, and several cooks tormented White. They refused to give him food, then they gave him garbage, and then they spat on his food. When he protested, he said, the cooks took him outside the mess hall and "beat the crap outta me."

Scared and enraged and unable to find his protective sergeant, he picked up a grenade launcher and went to the mess hall to kill the cooks, but no one was there. "So I blew up the mess hall."

After Dr. Bey submitted a medical report and the sergeant testified that White had shown good behavior before the crime, all charges were dropped, and he was returned to the United States.[157]

Mental health specialists throughout the war zone observed that Project 100,000 men were at high risk for psychiatric disturbances, according to Dr. Bey. "They were often the butt of jokes within their units," he said, and were tormented and scapegoated. If they were sent into a war zone (where enemies were actively trying to kill them), their level of stress increased dramatically, and they became overloaded with anxiety and dread. Some suffered from sleep problems, reduced appetite, loss of energy, irritability, and depression. Some were prone to lashing out (attacking other soldiers) or hurting themselves (attempting suicide or actually committing suicide).[158]

Dr. Bey tells of a 19-year-old draftee who was newly arrived in Vietnam. "His naïveté and overreaction to war stories made him a natural target for jokes and teasing in the unit. He was told, and believed, that the NVA [North Vietnamese Army] were going to launch an attack that would overrun and destroy his unit." He refused to eat, gave away his money and possessions, and talked about his imminent death. He inflicted deep wounds on his forehead and was taken to an evacuation hospital in Long Binh, where he evaded the medics and "climbed a sixty-foot tower, and jumped headfirst to the sidewalk below. He sustained serious injuries, including a broken neck. He miraculously survived his injuries and was evacuated back to the United States for further surgical and psychiatric treatment."[159]

In a study of intellectually disabled men at the mental hygiene clinic at the 67th Evacuation Hospital in Qui Nhon in a six-month period, two Army psychiatrists found that Project 100,000 soldiers were referred for psychiatric help *ten times* as frequently as other troops. "Project 100,000 men," they said, "seemed to have lowered stress tolerance, and a relative lack of the usual mechanisms for coping with stress."[160] In a separate study, four Army psychiatrists concluded, "Individuals of lower intellectual capacity have greater difficulty in adjustments than persons of average intelligence and thus more frequently become psychiatric problems or disciplinary offenders."[161]

Dr. Edward M. Colbach, an Army psychiatrist in Qui Nhon (1968-1969), tells the story of a young trooper he calls Danny, a Project 100,000 man who (says Colbach) never should have been in the military because of his intellectual deficiency. He was assigned to a support unit, where he had problems getting along with his sergeant. Dr. Colbach interviewed both Danny and the sergeant in an effort to bring about reconciliation. The sergeant, who was disgusted with Danny and other Project 100,000 men, "said that in his many years in the Army, he had never seen soldiers so inept. Some could hardly read or write. They seemed to have no emotional stamina, and extraordinary supervision was necessary to get them to complete a job."

Danny's sanity began to fall apart, and he became convinced that the sergeant was plotting to kill him. "Finally he became so agitated that he had to be admitted to the hospital in a panic state. We kept him in the hospital for a few days and settled him down on Thorazine [a powerful antipsychotic medication]."

One of the hospital's psychiatric technicians "strongly wanted to evacuate Danny. He was convinced that, in addition to his low intelligence, Danny had a thinking disorder." But Dr. Colbach decided against evacuating him to a larger hospital in Nha Trang or Japan. "Our evacuation quota for the month was just about used up. Because of this I convinced myself that Danny could be reintegrated into his unit." Unfortunately, a few nights later, Danny shot himself in the head with an M-16 rifle, and he died the next day.

Dr. Colbach felt remorse and guilt about the death of a man who should have been evacuated. Courageously admitting a mistake, he said that "Danny got a raw deal in life and he certainly got a raw deal in Vietnam. And I was part of it."[162]

At least one low-IQ man ended up as a prisoner of war in Vietnam. Rick Springman, a former POW held by the Viet Cong, told of a fellow prisoner who was one of McNamara's Boys. Hector Gonzalez (not his real name) "went crazy" in captivity. He defecated on himself all the time and had to be cleaned up by the other men. "He was retarded... it really pissed me off! Here was this retarded guy... and they'd sent him into a combat zone.... Hector would scream at the guards all the time [and they] would take him and make him stand on an anthill for a few hours. Or put him up against a tree in the sun for eight hours. They'd bring him back and Hector would start screaming again."[163]

# 29

# Crime and Punishment

U.S. Army Colonel Jack Crouchet, who was one of three military judges in Vietnam in 1968-69, noted that a number of Project 100,000 men stood trial for crimes committed in the war zone.

His first experience with "McNamara's Boys" involved Private Roy House (not his real name), who was charged with murder in the death of a fellow soldier. The circumstances were murky: House had been drinking beer with his comrades, an argument erupted, and one of the comrades lay dead. House said he had no memory of firing his weapon, but witnesses identified him as the one who pulled the trigger.

Colonel Crouchet said that House had grown up in poverty and was "subjected to the whims of an alcoholic father who was a poor provider." He repeated two grades and was unable to graduate from high school. He had always had a speech impediment. His only employment consisted of odd jobs. When the military summoned him to an induction center in 1967, he scored low on the AFQT but because of the lowered standards of Project 100,000, he was drafted into the Army.

Colonel Crouchet said that House's crime "could only have happened because of an unfortunate combination of circumstances: House's low intelligence and low regard for himself, the availability of weapons, the heat of the night, and the intensity of a war atmosphere." At his trial, a psychiatrist testified: "House's intelligence placed him in the mentally subnormal population. He has an emotionally unstable personality manifested by poorly controlled angry outbursts. His angry feelings overwhelm him. House was concealing, consciously or unconsciously, the true nature of his act because he cannot make sense out of what he did. Further, he lacks insights into his own intellectual dullness."

The psychiatrist found that "his general intellect seems uniformly dull and he is unable to make very simple abstractions. He cannot calculate how much change he would receive after purchasing something that costs less than a dollar but paying with a dollar.... He has experienced a lifelong pattern of being a scapegoat and inferior because of his gullibility, general dullness, and speech impediment."

The court gave House a dishonorable discharge and sentenced him to ten years "at hard labor" in a military prison. After the trial, Colonel Crouchet talked to House, "who showed little emotion or understanding of what had transpired. His stuttered sentences and lack of understanding convinced me that he should never have been allowed into military service." In fact, when he looked back at all of his court cases involving low-IQ men, he said, "In my own experience, I feel that every Project 100,000 soldier who was tried by general court-martial should not have been accepted into the armed forces."[164]

No one argued that a low level of intelligence excused a man from suffering the consequences of his wrongdoing, but in one trial involving a Project 100,000 man accused of participating in a prison riot, Colonel Crouchet quoted a defense attorney as saying, "The system that allows a person as unqualified as [the defendant] to join the Army and be sent to Vietnam is unjust.... The Army should bear some responsibility for recruiting young men who are totally unqualified to perform the tasks of a soldier."[165]

## 30

# Unfit for Combat,
# but He Wins a Silver Star

J im Bracewell, a helicopter pilot who commanded an air cavalry squadron in the Mekong Delta in 1970, tells the story of Mike Sanchez (not his real name), who "was a product of Project 100,000, or McNamara's Folly," and he never should have been sent to the war zone. "As soon as Mike was assigned to an infantry platoon in the field, the young lieutenant platoon leader realized that a terrible mistake had been made" and he requested that Mike be moved to a rear area. While the request was being processed, "Mike, a simple young man who could neither read nor write, remained in the infantry platoon [and was] asked to perform beyond his mental capabilities."

The platoon leader was very compassionate, and tried to keep Mike "under his wing," protecting him from ridicule "from unfeeling soldiers." In return, Mike developed an intense loyalty to the lieutenant. One day, as the platoon moved through some rice paddies, the men came under heavy fire from the enemy, and they ran for cover. "As soon as they reached cover, Mike looked for his lieutenant. He couldn't find him. He frantically began calling the platoon leader's name. One of the other soldiers told Mike to stop yelling, that he had seen the lieutenant go down, and he thought he was dead. Mike tearfully asked where he was. When he pinpointed the lieutenant's position, he shed his equipment (including his rifle) and ran through heavy fire to his lieutenant. He scrambled to his young leader's side, and discovered that he was badly hit in both legs."

Mike didn't know whether the lieutenant was dead or alive. "He made no attempt at first aid—it never occurred to him. He simply picked up the lieutenant as if he were a doll and ran back to the tree line. Neither of them were hit during their dash to the trees, and no one could believe it considering the intensity of enemy fire. They said the pattern of bullets hitting the rice paddy water all around them made it seem impossible that they were not hit. The lieutenant received first aid, and a short time later was evacuated by helicopter. He survived."

About a month later, Bracewell said, Mike was sent to a rear area to participate in a parade and receive a Silver Star for heroism, presented by the commanding general of his division. As was customary at ceremonies, the general presented the medal and then chatted with him for a few minutes. "It was during this chat that the general realized that something was not quite right," and he ordered his subordinates to remove Mike from combat.

Mike was assigned to the squadron commanded by Bracewell, who (along with his first sergeant) protected him for the rest of his year in Vietnam. With Bracewell's help, Mike dictated letters to his mother and sent her all of his pay except for ten dollars a month that he kept for himself. To keep him busy and give him a skill that he could use in civilian life, Bracewell and the first sergeant assigned him to the motor pool and tried to teach him to service vehicles, but "he failed miserably." Finally "we decided to make Mike my Jeep driver" even though he had never driven a vehicle in his life. "He actually did pretty well once he got used to the clutch. Even so, I did most of the driving. It was easier than trying to tell Mike where to take me. It became a source of local amusement around the camp to see the commanding officer doing the driving while the driver was perched in the commander's seat, grinning from ear to ear."

To help Mike plan for the future, Bracewell asked him what he wanted to do when he returned to civilian life. "He replied typically, 'I don't know, sir.' I pressed him. 'What would you like to do more than anything else?' He said, 'I want to be a barber. My brother is a barber, and I want to work for him.'"

Bracewell consulted the classified ads section of the *Army Times* and found several barber schools in or near Los Angeles, Mike's hometown. He corresponded with several schools until he found a barber school operated by a man who seemed sensitive to Mike's situation, and Bracewell urged Mike to follow up with the man when he returned home. Several years later, Bracewell learned that Mike had gone to the recommended barber school and was working as a barber with his brother.

In the summer of 2007, Bracewell learned that Mike had died. In a valedictory, Bracewell wrote, "If anything good ever came out of that time in our history, it was the good fortune that came Mike Sanchez' way. As it turned out for Mike, his being at the wrong place at the wrong time actually was the right place at the right time. He was a bona fide hero, and he shouldn't even have been there!"[166]


Mike Sanchez was not the only mentally limited man who was protected by his superiors. In the case of PFC White, described in the earlier chapter on "Going Crazy," Dr. Bey noted that "the kindness of the first sergeant [toward White] was a phenomenon I saw often during my military experiences." Such kindness was cited earlier in this book when I reported that a sergeant shielded Johnny Gupton from dangerous duties. In my research, I found other cases of low-IQ men being protected by their superiors. For example, George M. Watson, Jr., who served at the headquarters of the 101st Airborne Division in Vietnam from 1969 to 1970, remembers one of McNamara's Morons, a man who "had a good personality" but was "a loose cannon" and was never allowed to serve guard duty. He was assigned as a light-vehicle driver. "The first sergeant adopted him and made him a sort of company mascot," said Watson. "He managed to deliver packages and people, although there were some good stories about his getting lost when driving off the base." He was baffled by constant references to "down the road" and "up the road."[167]

Another low-IQ man whom a superior tried to protect was a soldier from Houston, Texas, identified as "Norman" in an article that appeared in the *Houston Chronicle*. Drafted after he finished special education school at age 20, Norman ended up in Vietnam and was fortunate to have a kind, protective platoon commander, who assigned him to work in the mess tent under the supervision of cooks. Everything seemed to go well until "a stray shell" killed Norman as he worked in the mess tent. One of the cooks was killed at the same time.[168]

One soldier profited from the compassion of a superior after he returned from Vietnam. His story was told on an Internet blog by a veteran who was a Spec 5 and senior company clerk for Headquarters Company at Fort Carson, Colorado, in 1970.

The Spec 5 remembered when the soldier, whom he called Harris, hobbled into his office to sign into the company. "I wondered why he was slightly bent over, walked with a cane, and looked like he was in pain." It turned out that Harris had gone through basic training and AIT and then was sent straight to Vietnam. "A few weeks after he got there, a mine damn near killed him. He spent a year in various hospitals" and then was sent back to the States for his last four months of regular duty.

"Harris needed his cane to walk, was in pain most of the time, and couldn't get out of bed on a rainy day. His back was still full of shrapnel, most of it in places where it couldn't be removed surgically. While I was wondering why the hell they hadn't discharged him, I glanced at his aptitude scores and froze. *Harris had a GT score of 68* [which was the equivalent of an IQ of 71, placing him in the lowest level, Category V, and making him ineligible for the draft]. The next morning I was having coffee with one of the personnel sergeants. I asked him if he had any idea what this guy was doing in the service. His short answer was: 'One of McNamara's Morons.' Then he explained [that] in 1966 Lyndon Johnson was facing a manpower shortage for his expanding war in Vietnam. It was not politically advisable to start cutting back on college deferments—too many of the parents were politically connected, and the body bags were starting to add up. The always efficient Robert McNamara devised a scheme that 'Would Provide Opportunity for the Less Fortunate.'"

A month later, Harris returned to the Spec 5's office, and "he had tears running down his face." Apparently the Army wanted to take back his combat pay because there were no orders in his file assigning him to Vietnam. "The Army had enlisted him, when he never should have been enlisted ... They'd sent him to Vietnam and gotten him blown up, leaving him crippled for life. They returned him to active duty when they should have given him an honorable discharge due to combat-related injuries and sent him home with a 100% disability check every month. Through all that, he'd managed to keep smiling. The Army telling him he wasn't supposed to have been there to begin with, it was his own fault he got blown up and he wasn't entitled to his lousy $130 in combat pay per month finally broke him."

Saying that "it takes a lot to leave me speechless," the Spec 5 wrote, "Did I happen to mention that Harris was black? [But] it wasn't really a matter of racial injustice, it was matter of Outright Injustice." The Spec 5 decided to take on the bureaucracy. He made many phone calls to try to persuade his superiors to intervene, and in the end, he triumphed. "Harris got to go home a couple months ahead of schedule. He kept his combat pay and Purple Heart, his discharge was a medical discharge due to combat-sustained injuries. ... He was also given 100% disability ... Not much to give a person in exchange for being crippled for life at nineteen years old."

The Spec 5, who identified himself as Grumpy on his Internet blog, was among the kind souls who helped Project 100,000 men in desperate circumstances.[169]

# Part Five

# *Unfit Men and Criminals*

# 31

# The Bottom of the Barrel

I n recalling the day in 1969 when he reported to the induction
center in downtown Cleveland, Ohio, for his pre-induction
exam, Mark Frutkin said, "At that point in the war they were
taking just about anyone they could get: misfits, flatfoots, the
half-crippled, and the half-crazed."[170]

His colorful description contained some truth. In the later
years of the war, the military began taking men with physical,
medical, moral, and psychological defects—men who were
often referred to as "the bottom of the barrel," or, in the words
of General Louis H. Wilson Jr., former Commandant of the
Marine Corps, "the dregs of society."[171]

Why were such men being taken? In a word, desperation.
The military was already inducting 354,000 McNamara's
Boys, as well as accepting volunteers (fewer and fewer as the
war dragged on) and drafting men who lacked exemptions (for
example, college students who were not attending school full-
time). But all of these men added together were not sufficient.
Thousands of additional men were urgently needed because of
three vexing circumstances:

First, there were many deaths and injuries in the war zone.
The years 1966 through 1971 were the "meat-grinder years,"
a grisly term used by some veterans. Most of the war's 58,220
dead and 321,704 wounded occurred during those years.[172]
The casualties left many units short-handed.

Second, thousands of soldiers were going AWOL or
deserting. The Senate Armed Services Committee said that in

1968 alone, absenteeism was costing the military the equivalent of ten combat divisions of 15,000 men each.[173]

Third, thousands of middle-class youths were avoiding the draft by using college deferments and other loopholes.

Where could the military find extra manpower? Johnson and his advisors could have changed their policy of not sending college boys and National Guardsmen and Reservists to Vietnam, but once again they wanted to avoid displeasing middle-class voters. So they solved the problem in two ways:

1. Induction centers had a monthly quota for how many Project 100,000 men they could take. When they used up their quota, they were instructed to continue to take low-scoring men but not count them as part of Project 100,000. In this way, thousands of additional low-IQ men were brought into the ranks.[174] In one case, according to a U.S. government report, a man was inducted even though he had an IQ of 69 (in the supposedly ineligible Category V) and a limited educational background—*he was 14 years old when he completed the third grade.*[175]

2. Recruiters and induction centers were pressured to cast a wider net and bring in thousands of additional men who would normally fail to qualify for military duty—men with health problems, physical defects, psychological disorders, criminal backgrounds, and alcohol or drug addiction. These "second-class fellows" (to use President Johnson's term) served a political goal: they spared healthier, wealthier men in the middle class from being drafted.

Many military commanders lamented the skewed priorities that put playing politics ahead of creating a high-quality fighting force. Adrian R. Lewis, a retired U.S. Army major who taught at West Point, said, "The primary concern of the draft was pacification of the American people, to disrupt American society as little as possible. Providing the Armed Forces with the best men possible was, at best, a secondary consideration."[176]

# 32

# "If You Can Breathe, You're In"

As the military grew more and more desperate for manpower, induction centers grabbed every warm body they could find—even men with serious medical conditions such as asthma, high blood pressure, and hearing loss.[177]

Surprisingly, induction centers were sometimes oblivious to the importance of effective fingers. One Army veteran said, "I went to basic training with a guy who had lost two fingers on his right hand. They told him that as long as he had his trigger finger, he could go to war."[178] War correspondent Gloria Emerson remembered "the pale boy who had lost the top of his index finger in a farm accident but was drafted anyway and expected to use a rifle."[179] James G. Miles, who commanded a basic training company at Fort Jackson, South Carolina, in 1967, was dismayed by the low caliber of men being inducted. He told of one trainee who had, as a child, suffered severe burns to his upper torso and arms. "As a result, the fingers of his right hand were fused together. He couldn't pull the trigger on a rifle. Because of burn injuries to his neck, he had trouble turning his head." Miles said that the medical officer who had examined him at an induction center "should have been court-martialed."[180]

James Lafferty, an attorney in Detroit, Michigan, and a draft counselor, explained that "the examining process at the induction stations bore absolutely no resemblance to the Mayo Clinic or any other legitimate health facility. They were cattle calls. Yes, there were doctors there, but their goal was to process as many people as possible. Day in and day out, people who had legitimate ailments under the written regulations put forth by the Selective Service System were approved for military service."[181]

At one induction center, a doctor landed in hot water after he refused to go along with the "draft-'em-all" approach. Dr. Walter Emory, who had been a staff sergeant in the Air National Guard during the Korean War, worked in the Phoenix, Arizona, induction center for four years until he was fired in May, 1970, because he disqualified a number of young men who had medical problems such as gout, diabetes, kidney abnormalities, and heart defects. Dr. Emory declined to march in step with other doctors at the induction center, who (he said) systematically overlooked areas of the body (such as knees and back), which most often have disqualifying defects. The purpose of the induction centers, said Dr. Emory, was supposed to be screening out men not qualified for the armed services. "However," he told a newspaper reporter in 1970, "this purpose has been distorted. Every inductee who comes in is seen as a malingering hippie. The inductee has to present proof of any defects. It actually turns into a contest between the inductee and the doctors. Unfortunately, the doctor usually wins because he can ignore the evidence."[182]

Staff Sergeant Bill Adams, who was a drill instructor at Fort Bliss, Texas, in 1969-1970, said that he saw medical problems in some of the trainees in his various basic training platoons. He remembered one man who was blind in one eye (he had an artificial eye). Another had a speech impediment that was so severe he could not make himself understood (he ended up communicating by writing notes). Several men had difficulty hearing unless you shouted into an ear. Adams said that efforts to have the men medically discharged were rebuffed—presumably because the Army was reluctant to send anyone home at a time of manpower shortages in Vietnam.[183]

In a three-year period (1968 -1970), the military accepted an estimated 60,000 men who should have been rejected for physical defects, according to the Government Accountability Office, a federal agency that audits and investigates government activities.[184]

"They were drafting anyone who could breathe," said David Caruso, academic vice president at Worcester State College in Massachusetts, who was drafted in 1966. "That's why I was taken [despite having flat feet and a serious back problem]. They were taking anybody. There were people in my basic training company who had permanent limps."[185]

A permanent limp was not just a minor abnormality. Marine Sergeant John L. Ward remembered that in boot camp, Private Woods "walked as though his feet were hurting. As time went on, our platoon mates and I were aware of the awkward gait of his every step, especially when he had to run. When we were on a ten-mile run, he could not carry on alone. Private Goldstone and I had to assist him by putting his arms over our shoulders and grabbing his belt on both sides.... He was able to graduate from boot camp, and was sent off to the combat arena."[186]

Ward also remembered a recruit who "was almost blind and could not see the target to test at the rifle range."[187] At a Chicago induction center in 1972, Patrick Murfin said he was deemed physically acceptable "despite my dismal eyesight—I was 20-200 in one eye and completely un-functional without my thick glasses."[188] Joel S. Franks, a veteran, says that in his basic training squad in 1969, "there was a trucker from Richmond named Bragg who was blind in one eye and deaf in one ear."[189]

Carlos Martinez, who says he "grew up on the streets and in the orphanages of Bronx and Brooklyn," was rejected by the military in 1964 as physically unfit for service. But in 1967, lo and behold, he was now fit. "We were the bottom of the barrel," he said. "I was almost legally blind. But when we got down to the induction station in 1967, it really wasn't about the physicals, man, it was like you were being taken. The assumption was already made that you were available. Everybody was taken. The only way you don't pass is if you don't have a leg."[190]

George Buford, the Anchorage induction center testing official discussed earlier, said that at most induction centers, "the physicals were a joke; if the meat was still hanging on your bones and your body was at least room temperature, you were declared fit for military service."[191]

Veterans like Buford laugh when they hear some men (who were military age in the 1960s) say later that they had wanted to fight in Vietnam but were turned away. (For example, Congressman Tom DeLay of Texas said that so many minority youths had volunteered, "there was literally no room for patriotic folks like myself."[192]) Buford noted that if you had gone to a recruiter and said you wanted to serve, "the recruiter would have smiled and started filling out the paperwork. Medical problems? No problem; the recruiter would show you how to hide them. Criminal record? No problem; the recruiter would show you how to hide it. Dumb as snot? Minor problem, but many recruiters had copies of the intelligence test they could use to prepare you with the right answers. In short, unless you were severely and obviously disabled, you could easily arrange to get into the military and be sent to Vietnam. Anyone who says otherwise is a liar."[193]

# 33

# Too Heavy, Too Thin, Too Short

A mong the ranks of the Armed Forces in 1966-1971 were men who had been unacceptable because of their body size—for example, too heavy, too thin, or too short—until Project 100,000 suddenly made them fair game. (As I reported earlier, nine percent of Project 100,000 men were accepted because of new, less stringent physical standards.) Because they were "different," these men were often harassed and given humiliating names—overweight men were ridiculed with such names as Fatty, Lard Ass, and Porky; excessively thin men, Skin-and-Bones, and tiny men, Runt and Midget.

Before 1966, some chubby men were taken into the military, but they were not grossly overweight and many of them said later that they were glad that they were forced into physical exertion so that they could shed weight and get into shape. But with McNamara's new standards, men were accepted who could only be described as obese.

From 1966 to 1971, it seemed as if every other basic training company had at least one obese trainee, often the recipient of terrible abuse. In his first day in basic training at Fort Bliss, Texas, in 1969, Peter Tauber saw a company pass by, "running in step as a drill sergeant calls cadence.... Twenty yards behind them a whale of a recruit stumbles forward, lurching to keep up, falling further behind. On his tail is a small, slight drill sergeant.... The fat boy runs a jagged route, spinning to his right and his left as he goes, his head lolling from side to side, drooling and wearing an expression of imminent death. From time to time, he closes his eyes, as if to pray for a merciful tumble. Fifty yards past us he falls. We can hear the sergeant yelling at him as he wallows on the ground.... But the fat boy, who must weigh what two of us do, just lies there. The sergeant yells some more and tries to pull him up. The next thing we hear is a scream. The sergeant is standing over the fallen boy and is kicking him in the stomach and backside, sometimes prodding, sometimes letting go with a field-goal kick. Screaming sobs fill the air, wails of torture and pain. The sergeant takes off his pistol belt and begins to whip his prey. The boy holds up his hands to protect his face and the sergeant kicks them away. The boy pleads, then cries and screams for the sergeant to stop, but the sergeant keeps beating him." Eventually, the sergeant relents and lets the trainee get up and rejoin his platoon.[194]

Such abuse caused some overweight men to become deeply depressed. Army veteran John Ketwig tells of a trainee called "Fatso" at Fort Dix, New Jersey, who committed suicide after suffering horrendous cruelty at the hands of a sadistic sergeant. "Once, he had been a law student," said Ketwig. "He had been called to do his duty. He had a wife."[195]

Writer Jack Todd recalled an episode that took place during Marine training at Camp Upshur in Virginia in 1967. "When a fat trainee fell out on a training run, three sergeants surrounded him and kicked him in the stomach until he puked."[196]

Meanwhile, at the other end of the weight spectrum were men who had previously been rejected for being excessively thin. Some of them had a hard time with the rigors of training because they were too puny to carry heavy loads of equipment, while other super-thin men fared well. For example, at the Marine boot camp in San Diego, underweight men were told to go through the chow lines twice, according to James Westheider, who cites a recruit named Gerald Kumpf, who was six feet tall and only 136 pounds when he entered the Marine

Corps. By the end of boot camp, he had gained nearly 50 pounds, weighing about 185 pounds.[197]

Thanks to Robert McNamara, some inductees were extremely short. Dr. Lawrence William, the Army doctor quoted earlier, tells an incredible story about a tiny man inducted under the new Project 100,000 physical standards: "One day, I was in the little Quonset hut [at Dong Tam] that served as my dispensary seeing the morning sick call. A very little person wearing a somewhat baggy private's uniform walked in to see me. 'What seems to be the problem, private?' I asked. 'This, sir,' he replied, with an abnormally high-pitched voice. With that comment he gave his foot a flick and the too-large boot that had been on it flew off and bounced off the wall of my Quonset hut. 'Sir, my shoe size is 4½. I can take a size 5 in a pinch. But, sir, I have heard that the smallest boot they have in the Army is 6 and this size 7 they issued to me will not stay on my feet!'"

When Smithson (not his real name) entered the Army, he measured below the official 4' 8" minimum height, but the Army was desperate for bodies of any size. Each time he was given a uniform, said Dr. William, "it was way too big for him.... And every time he complained about his uniform not fitting, they reassured him that the Army would deal with this problem once he reached his permanent duty station. Dong Tam was his permanent duty station. He wanted me to get him the boots he needed." Smithson was supposed to become an Army cook. "However, he was too short to reach to the top of the military range and way too short to stir one of the large pots used to cook the Army meals. His boots were too big to be worn safely and his uniform hung on him as if he were, well, a dwarf. Well, what could one expect? I asked myself; he is a dwarf!"

Although the soldier did not have the "abnormal bodily proportions" associated with dwarfism, Dr. William diagnosed him as a dwarf in order to get him out of the Army. Dr. William found that he had to follow correct Army procedures, which turned out to be ludicrous when applied to this situation. "I completed a field medical tag, the first step in this process, which attested to the fact that he was being medevaced because he was a dwarf. He was instructed to lie on one of the canvas litters available for the wounded. 'Can't I just walk out?' he asked. 'Nope, regulations say that if you are to be evacuated, you must lie on the gurney and take off your boots and socks.' I twisted the soft wire tie of the field medical tag around Private Smithson's great toe on his bare right foot. After a short wait, the ambulance I had requested arrived and he was then evacuated from my aid station to the 3rd Surgical Hospital nearby in Dong Tam. There they confirmed that he was still a dwarf and that they were unable to cure this problem! Therefore, they evacuated him by helicopter to the 93rd Evaluation Hospital in Long Binh. From Long Binh, he was medevaced to the 93rd Field Hospital in Saigon. Then he was transported by plane to Japan. They, too, could not cure his dwarfism and so he was transported by plane to Tripler Army Hospital in Hawaii. Once again they were unable to cure his problem and so he was separated from the Army in Hawaii. To this day, Smithson has a service-connected disability, since this disability was 'discovered' while he was on active duty in a war zone. He is therefore entitled to complete medical benefits for life in any Veterans Affairs Hospital in the United States."

Years later, Dr. William said, he was still shaking his head in disbelief about "the insanity of drafting a dwarf and then needing to separate him from the military as if he were war-wounded."[198]

# 34

# Criminals

For many NCOs and officers, the Pentagon policy that caused the most anger and outrage in the later years of the war was the relaxation of so-called "moral standards." Men who had been convicted of serious crimes (like armed robbery) were supposed to be disqualified from service, but recruiters and induction centers were given the authority to grant "moral waivers" to bring them into the ranks. In a common scenario, a judge, working in collaboration with a recruiter, would give a young offender a choice—go to jail or join the Army or Marine Corps.[199] (This was what happened to Jeff Hardin, the petty criminal whom I described in Part Two.) During the war, Nick D'Allesandro of Utica, New York, went west to join a Hell's Angels motorcycle gang near Anaheim, California. One day he chain-whipped a truck driver, and a judge gave him a choice: join the Army or go to jail. He chose the Army and ended up serving in Vietnam as a Green Beret. He later admitted that in interrogations he tortured Vietnamese men and women with electric shocks applied to their genitals.[200]

In many cases, judges felt that military service would help a man to straighten up, develop self-discipline, and become a functioning citizen. But not everyone was happy about the procedure. Congressman Charles Wilson of Texas said, "We have evidence that law authorities are more or less happy to get rid of their problems and to throw them off on the Army or the Marine Corps or the Navy."[201] William Westmoreland, commanding general of U.S. Forces in Vietnam (1964-1968), bitterly denounced the "enlist or go to jail" policy because it caused the induction of men "with a penchant for trouble" and led to serious morale and discipline problems during the later years of the war.[202]

"Most officers and NCOs believed that [criminals] made poor soldiers," noted historian James Westheider. "Individuals that cannot obey the rules and regulations of civilian society could hardly be expected to accept and conform to the much more rigid discipline and expectations of the Armed Forces."[203]

When a judge and a recruiter worked out a deal, the procedure was known as "punitive enlistment." Some men who had racked up police records in civilian life did well in the military, but some did not.[204] Gonzalo Baltazar, who fought in the 2nd Battalion of the 17th Division, said that several men in his battalion had been granted punitive enlistments. While he was a civilian, one man had used his car to deliberately run over and kill someone. Despite the serious nature of the crime, a judge gave him the option of jail or Vietnam. He chose Vietnam, but he "did not work out." He "snapped and he couldn't handle the combat." He eventually went AWOL.[205]

Dr. Douglas Bey, mentioned earlier as a combat psychiatrist for the 1st Infantry Division in Vietnam, tells of one unpopular soldier, a troublemaker who had entered the Army after being told by a judge that he could choose jail or military service. "His infantry unit in Vietnam made him a point man [walking at the front of his platoon while on patrol], hoping to get rid of him." He survived walking point, but was later imprisoned after he murdered an NCO.[206]

No statistics are available on how many men with criminal records were inducted during the war, but the number may have been substantial because many veterans reported having the same experience as Michael Volkin, a trainee at Fort Leonard Wood, who said he was a "typical white suburban kid, and a lot of the people I went through basic with were there in answer to the simple question, 'Would you rather be in the Army or in jail?'"[207]

Criminal behavior was often accompanied by alcohol and drug abuse. If a man had a police record for drunk driving or intoxicated assaults, he would have been rejected in the days before the Vietnam War. But after the war began, because of manpower shortages, he was accepted. Juan Ramirez of San Francisco, a Marine veteran who was arrested for drunk driving and assault after he returned home from the war, admitted that "my problems stemmed from being an alcoholic and violent long before going to Vietnam."[208]

Some men had experienced severe psychiatric disturbances in their civilian lives. Military historian Keith William Nolan tells the distressing story of PFC Michael Monk (not his real name) of the 31st Infantry Division who went berserk one night at Firebase Smoke near Saigon in 1968. Shouting incoherently, he sprayed bullets randomly at his comrades, killing three of them. An investigation revealed that "Monk had been under psychiatric care before being drafted." If his induction center had carefully examined his civilian record, he would have been identified as "a dangerously unstable individual" who should not have been admitted into the Armed Forces.[209]

P. J. Rice, an Army attorney in Germany and Vietnam, remembered a young soldier who was wild and disorderly. "I was in Germany from 1966 to 1969. For part of that period, I was a 4th Armored Division defense counsel. I got to know some of Secretary McNamara's boys. One, whose name was Jake, got in trouble about every other week. He should have kept me on a retainer. I kept getting him out of trouble, but I wasn't sure that was to his benefit. A separation from the Army would have been better. First, Jake got drunk and started a fight in a local *gasthaus* [tavern]. It was a tough place and there was plenty of blame to spread around. Later, Jake beat up a German taxi driver. He claimed the driver pulled a weapon on him (probably because Jake refused to pay for the ride). I won't elaborate on the many times he missed formations and was disrespectful to officers and NCO's. The last time I saw Jake was when he came by to thank me and tell me he was on orders to Vietnam. His arm was in a sling. I had to ask. He said, 'Oh that, it happened when I flipped the jeep.'... I thought long and hard about whether I should notify someone. I wasn't concerned about him hurting himself, but what about the soldiers in his unit? What about the cab drivers in Saigon?"[210]

In the final years of the war, men who were violent, angry, or disturbed became a significant presence in the Army and Marine Corps, and according to many officers, they were responsible for a serious breakdown of discipline among the troops in Vietnam. In 1971, Colonel Robert D. Heinl wrote in *Armed Forces Journal*, "Our Army that now remains in Vietnam is in a state approaching collapse, with individual units avoiding or having refused combat, murdering their officers, drug-ridden, and dispirited where not near-mutinous."[211]

According to Baskir and Strauss, "The most serious symptom of the crisis in discipline in Vietnam was 'fragging,' real or threatened assaults on officers and high-ranking sergeants." The practice got its name from "fragmentation grenade," which could be rolled into the area where an officer or NCO was sleeping. When it exploded, no fingerprints could be found. The target was often a leader who was hated because he was incompetent in leading men, or excessively harsh in his discipline, or overly aggressive in waging war (putting the lives of soldiers and Marines at unnecessary risk just so that he could gain glory and advance his own career).[212]

In addition to thousands of threats that were never carried out, there were confirmed reports of at least 800 fraggings or attempted fraggings in the Army and Marine Corps, with 86 men killed and an estimated 700 wounded.[213] "But this was probably only the tip of a deadly iceberg," according to historian Westheider. The true figure may never be known. Many officers felt unsafe simply because they were authority figures. During his second tour in Vietnam at Duc Pho in 1968-1969, Major Colin Powell (later a four-star general) said he was "living in a large tent and I moved my cot every night, partly to thwart Viet Cong informants who might be tracking me, but also because I did not rule out attacks on authority from within the battalion itself." Captain Thomas Cecil, who was stationed at Cam Ranh Bay in 1970-1971, "was so worried about attacks on his life that during his last month in Vietnam, he slept in the military intelligence (MI) bunker, and only his battalion commander knew where he was at night."[214]

Among Marines in 1968, fragging was a worse problem than illegal drug use, according to a team of Marine Corps historians, who wrote that although the number of fraggings was relatively small, "the knowledge that fraggings occurred often had a chilling effect on a leader's willingness to enforce discipline."[215]

Army veteran George Lepre's book-length investigation of hundreds of fraggings *(Fragging: Why U.S. Soldiers Assaulted Their Officers in Vietnam)* found that most of the attacks occurred after dark in Army and Marine Corps units—they were rare in the Air Force and Navy. Innocent bystanders sometimes became "the unintended victims of the attacks," and the families of fragging victims usually were not given the true details of what had happened to the deceased.[216]

Most fraggings occurred inside camps, while out in jungles and rice paddies, a different method was used by infantrymen who wanted to kill "bad officers," according to Robert Nylen, the combat infantry officer quoted earlier. "Sometimes, an errant bullet struck an incompetent fool amid a firefight. Problem solved."[217]

# 35

# Misfits

During the war, an Army private named Paul Solo was quoted as saying, "The Army keeps a lot of strange dudes off the street."[218] The most common examples of "strange dudes" were known in the military as "misfits" —chronically maladaptive soldiers who were unable to fit in with other soldiers because they were disturbingly different from everyone else. "Misfits," wrote author Peter Barnes, "tend to share a number of common characteristics. A large majority are high school dropouts [who are] often slow-witted loner types who are not particularly attractive or likable. In civilian life, most of them have been losers many times over. In the military, this pattern is repeated."[219]

In times when the military is not desperate for warm bodies, misfits are turned away. One effective screening device is to reject high school dropouts—a policy used by the Armed Forces whenever possible (on the supposition that if a man drops out of high school, he is unlikely to possess enough self-discipline to perform well in the military). If misfits manage to slip through pre-induction screening and they enter basic training, their inability to adapt becomes noticeable, and they are usually discharged, sometimes with a diagnosis of "personality disorder." But during the Vietnam War, misfits were kept because of manpower shortages. Most of them were poor learners or slow adjusters, they were unable to make friends, and they became targets of their superiors' rage and their peers' resentment.[220] Malcolm Miller-Jones, a veteran who grew up in New York City, noted that "group cohesion" was important for platoons in training and in combat, and a man who failed to work in sync with his comrades and failed to do his share of the chores was often the recipient of a blanket party, in which a blanket was thrown over the man, and his platoon mates beat him anonymously with their fists. A blanket party would cause some men to shape up and become cooperative, but it failed to reform others.[221]

Kyle Benson, who was an artillery NCO in Vietnam, gave me a description of a misfit in his basic training company at Fort Jackson, South Carolina, in 1968. "I was a squad leader, and one guy in my squad was sullen and anti-social. He never engaged in small talk with anyone. Never laughed at the jokes, never participated in the silly banter that filled the barracks in the evenings as we shined our boots and got ready for the next day. He wouldn't pull his load. He would disappear when he was supposed to be on a work detail with other men. Once I ordered him to clean the toilets in the latrine, but he ducked out halfway through the job. So the next time, I stood over him and watched him, but he did a half-ass job. I hated him. So did everyone else. He was sloppy in getting his bunk and locker ready for inspection, and this sometimes caused the whole platoon to be punished. One night the platoon gave him a blanket party—he got beat up pretty bad. But he didn't change his ways. In the old days, he would have been given a dishonorable discharge, but because of Vietnam, the Army kept him. He passed basic, but I don't know what happened to him after that."[222]

A type of misfit who aroused a great deal of resentment was the malingerer, who shirked his duties by claiming illness or incapacity. Columnist Tom Halsted tells of an event that occurred while he was a lieutenant in the Panama Canal Zone. Although the event occurred in 1955 (four years before the first U.S. casualties in Vietnam), it offers a timeless portrait of a malingering misfit in the U.S. Army: "One Saturday I was assigned to lead a motley group of soldiers into the jungle near our base at Fort Kobbe, up over Cerro Galera, a nearby low mountain, down the other side and back to the base.... One of the group was a loner and a misfit. Friendless and nearly impossible to befriend, Private Billy Boggs (not his real name) was the classic sad sack. Unable or unwilling to learn even the most basic tasks, clumsy, late for everything, he was a constant trial for his fellow soldiers, endlessly exasperating his squad leader and platoon sergeant, and certainly me, his platoon leader. He really didn't belong in the Army, certainly not in the infantry, where we all knew that if we ever faced combat we could be in situations where we would have to depend on each other for our safety, perhaps for our lives. Nobody had the slightest confidence that Boggs would be there when anyone needed him."

Thirty minutes after the soldiers started up the mountainside, said Halsted, "I heard a crash and a clatter of falling equipment behind me and called a halt. Near the end of the column, Boggs had collapsed by the side of the trail, his equipment all around him, and gasped that he could go no further. His squad leader tried to drag him to his feet, and he fell back to the ground, rubber-legged, his face ashen, and his fatigues soaked with sweat. His helmet and rifle lay in the mud beside him."

Halsted knew that Boggs had gone on sick call for three straight days, and each time, he had been sent back to duty with no signs of illness. So the lieutenant ordered Boggs to get up and keep climbing. "Can't, Lieutenant," he groaned. "I'm sick." For the remainder of the hike, Halsted and the rest of the men took turns carrying Boggs on their shoulders. He was "a soggy, uncooperative burden... who stank—of sweat, of urine, of who knew what. And he wouldn't stop groaning. Or sweating. At least he wasn't wetting his pants anymore. I hoped."

The men spent a grueling day hiking up and down the mountain, carrying the "sorry, sweat-stained malingerer." Finally, in the evening, they returned to the barracks, and Halsted dismissed them. "Boggs slipped off his latest porter's shoulders and, amazingly rejuvenated, almost trotted back to his quarters."[223]

## 36

# Who Was Who?

B ecause of the motley variety of substandard men who were taken into the Armed Forces during the war, it became difficult to place them into neat categories. For example, how could you identify who was officially a member of Project 100,000 and who was not? In the early years of Project 100,000, a service number that began with "67" signified that an individual was in the program.[224] But in later years, when service numbers were replaced by Social Security numbers, there was no such easy identifier.[225]

Some officers and sergeants tried to determine if a man had an intellectual disability by looking at his personnel record. If he had scored low—Category IV—on the Armed Forces Qualification Test, he would have qualified to enter the service under Project 100,000, but there were two complicating factors: (1) men who scored in the upper level of Category IV had normal or close-to-normal intelligence, and (2) some of the men who scored in the middle and lower levels of Category IV were not mentally limited—they scored poorly because they spoke a language other than English, had dyslexia, were illiterate, or lacked test-taking skills.

And then there was the question of how to categorize the other "second-class fellows"—men who had been rated as too heavy, too thin, or too short under previous standards, and men with medical liabilities, psychiatric disorders, criminal tendencies, or maladjustment problems.

All of these labels caused a lot of confusion in terminology. When some veterans and commentators talked about McNamara's Morons, they used the term as an umbrella for *all* substandard men—not just men with intellectual disabilities. For example, in 1968 an officer with the Americal Division requested that a percentage limit be placed on the number of Project 100,000 men placed in the division. He complained that the men had "difficulty in job performance" and some of them "exhibited criminal behavior."[226] He was making an assumption that many people made: any serviceman who screwed up—either mentally or morally—was one of McNamara's Morons. But this was technically incorrect: Just because a man injected heroin or committed violent crimes, he was not necessarily a part of Project 100,000. Maybe he was, but maybe he wasn't.

In reporting the stories told by officers, NCOs, and comrades, the best I can do is to convey what these veterans remembered about substandard men from October, 1966, through December, 1971—even if there were probably some instances of mislabeling.

Ultimately, assigning substandard men to different categories is not as important as recognizing that most of them belonged to one big grouping: Men who never should have been taken into the Armed Forces.

# Part Six

# *Winners and Losers*

# 37

# Success Stories

A number of Project 100,000 men were successful in the military. Most of them were "street smart" men whose test scores placed them in the higher level of Category IV, but there were also some success stories among men whose intellectual deficits caused them to test in the lower level of the category.

Chief Hospital Corpsman Don Phelps of Oxnard, California, who was in charge of a "rather large sick bay" on a Navy ship, recalled an assistant, Elmer (not his real name), who was assigned to him over his objections. Phelps wanted his sick bay to be immaculately clean so that it would "out-shine and out-show any and all spaces aboard." He didn't want to take on Elmer as an assistant "because he was one of McNamara's Boys and he had no schooling and no chances of a responsible job in later life." Furthermore, he was "not too bright" and "he had to be taught the concepts of 'clean' and 'sterile.'"

But Phelps was ordered to take Elmer, and he was immediately surprised by the young man's solid performance and eagerness to please. Elmer made the sick bay sparkle with cleanliness. Phelps said, "I couldn't have asked for a cleaner, sharper space if I had a crew of five working for me." Because of Elmer's mental limitations, Phelps said, he never gave him "any large amount of detailed work," but in the basic cleaning jobs that he assigned, "Elmer took extreme pride in what he did accomplish." He was "very polite and developed a highly commendable appearance."

By tackling the "dirty work" and doing it exceptionally well, Elmer "relieved hard-pressed lab, x-ray, and operating room techs to perform their functions more efficiently." He was vastly superior to the assistants of normal intelligence that Phelps had worked with—men who were sloppy and had a bad attitude.[227]

The story of Elmer supports the argument—made by many educators and psychologists—that low-aptitude individuals can be productive in low-stress, non-dangerous situations. Here is another such example:

While serving as a lieutenant in the 9th Infantry Division in the Mekong Delta, Jack Durish spent six months as the division's casualty reporting officer, sending letters of condolence to the next of kin of men who had been killed in combat. Three different letters had to be sent—one each from the unit commander, the division chaplain, and the commanding general—and most of the time, the letters had to be ghostwritten by Durish.

"Every letter had to be typewritten perfectly," he said. "Erasures were equally forbidden along with errors. We feared that the next of kin might interpret any error as evidence that we could have made other mistakes, such as misidentified the remains, and that the person in the [sealed] casket might not be their loved one. Interestingly, my best typist was a young man who seemingly should never have been drafted or recruited. His mental acuity was severely disabled. However, he was diligent in his duties, never distracted, and rarely made an error.... I wish I had more like him."[228]

For some Project 100,000 men, military service was a welcome opportunity for excitement, travel, and self-improvement. Harry N. Watkins of Enka, North Carolina, was a good example of the kind of soldier who scored low on intelligence tests but nevertheless had plenty of savvy.

Watkins won promotion to sergeant for an ingenious procedure he introduced at Fort Dix, New Jersey, in 1971. His job was to help process troops for overseas duty. Before he arrived, the cadre were having trouble keeping track of all the men who were supposed to fly out. Some of the men would go AWOL for an evening (for one last stateside fling) and ask a buddy to answer when their names were called at formations. When Watkins had to verify who was present, he called out the last four digits of a man's Social Security number. The "buddy," not knowing this information, was unable to answer, so the absence was immediately detected.

Watkins' ploy was not originally intended to catch AWOLs. He simply could not read the men's names. He was illiterate, and he used the Social Security gimmick to conceal his problem. He did this sort of thing all through his stay in the Army. "I was so ashamed for anybody to know that I couldn't read," he said. When forms had to be filled out, he would complain about not having his glasses and ask someone else to do the reading and writing for him.

Watkins was unable to read not because he was dull but because he never had a chance to learn. "I grew up in a very poor part of the North Georgia mountains," he said. "We were so poor our knees stuck through our britches. We just didn't have time nor money for school. I had to help the family."

When he went to an induction center to take the AFQT in 1969, he told the testers that he was unable to read, but they told him to go through the answer sheet and fill in a blank at random beside each number. Thanks to the lowering of standards by Project 100,000, this method could yield a score high enough to qualify for military service.

Watkins was sent to Vietnam, where he worked at the Cat Lai port on the Saigon River, supervising the unloading of heavy cases from ammunition ships. After 10 months, he suffered a back injury, and was transferred to Fort Dix to finish out his service time doing light, clerical work. "I really liked the Army, and I wanted to stay in, but they wouldn't let me because of my back." After discharge, his back problem got worse, and he spent many months at the Veterans Affairs Hospital in Oteen, North Carolina, which is where I met him and interviewed him. The forced idleness gave him an incentive to learn to read. "I got bored just lying on my back all day. I'd always wanted to be able to read the Word of God." So he worked on reading the Bible. "I got over being embarrassed. I'd ask the nurses and orderlies to help me sound out words." One thing that helped him was knowing large portions of the Bible by heart. He had heard preachers recite certain verses so often that he was able to quote them perfectly. When it came to reading the Bible, it was like seeing an old friend in a new way.

Although his back injury kept him from working in his field (carpentry), he became a part-time Pentecostal preacher. "The Lord is using me to heal the sick and the lame," he said. He was not bitter about being drafted and becoming disabled. "It was the Lord's will. I got to travel clear over to the other side of the world. I made a lot of friends, I got paid good, I got promoted to buck sergeant. I'd wanted to stay in the Army, but the Lord had other plans for me. When I was flat on my back in the hospital, it was for a purpose. The Lord was saying, 'You've been moving too fast. Now it's time to slow down and take time to read My Word.' Everything has a purpose. The Lord knows best."[229]

Next is a story of success that was clouded by a propensity for violence. Major Ronald J. Ellefson, who was commander of an armor battalion in 1967-69, presided over the court martial of a Project 100,000 man who pleaded guilty to stabbing another soldier in the arm because the other man was "always picking on me and calling me names." The court sentenced the attacker to six months in the stockade. "As was customary," said Major Ellefson, "two weeks later I visited him in the stockade. He was tearful, apologetic, and told me that he had written to his mother about what he had done. When I asked him what he wanted to do when he got out of jail, he said that he would like to be a jeep driver."

A week or two later, Ellefson needed a new driver, and he arranged for the young man to receive a reduced sentence and return to the unit. "I assigned him as my driver, but beforehand, I told this soldier exactly what I expected. I warned him that a repeat performance with a knife would not only put him back in jail, but the next time, we'd throw the key away."

Ellefson said that the soldier "turned out to be a tremendous driver. Always on time when needed, took excellent care of the maintenance, and kept the jeep better polished than most staff cars. After he had proven to be so hard-working, conscientious, and reliable, I wrote his mother a letter and told her what a fine job he was doing."

When it came time for the soldier to leave the unit, Ellefson gave him a few days off to take care of his personal business. But a sergeant reported that he walked into the enlisted men's club and "found my driver waving a pocket knife at a number of other soldiers. It was a tense situation and when the sergeant asked my driver what he was up to, he was told 'get the hell away, I'm going to get me some of these wise asses.' The sergeant told me that all he could think of to say was 'I'm going to tell the Major about you.' The driver said, 'Oh, god no,' threw down the knife and ran back to his barracks."

Ellefson decided not to take any action against the driver, and he let him leave for his next duty station.[230]

# 38

# Absent Without Leave

The major illegality in the Armed Forces during the Vietnam War was absenteeism—AWOL (an absence of less than 30 days) and desertion (30 days or longer). "During the entire period of the Vietnam War," say Baskir and Strauss, "there were approximately 1,500,000 AWOL incidents and 500,000 desertion incidents. At the peak of the war in 1968, an American soldier was going AWOL every two minutes, and deserting every six minutes."[231] In 1970 alone, wrote Marine Colonel Robert D. Heinl Jr., "the Army had 65,643 deserters, or roughly the equivalent of four infantry divisions."[232]

According to writer Peter Barnes, most of the absentees were "young and often immature" soldiers who went AWOL out of "boredom, fatigue, homesickness, desire to see a girlfriend back home, anxiety over a young wife, worry over ill or destitute parents…trouble with paychecks and allotments, debts for purchases [they] could not afford, and the very common inability to handle two problems with which [they] had little experience before coming into the Army—women and liquor."[233]

Project 100,000 men were more likely than other soldiers to run away.[234] Often their behavior stemmed from their personal and family history. Many of the men grew up in poor families, with no father present, and they had little or no education, but lots of chaos and confusion in their homes and neighborhoods.[235]

For some low-IQ men, running away was a common response to stress and harassment. They failed to stop and ponder the many warnings they had heard throughout their time in the military—warnings of the dire consequences of going AWOL or deserting. They were told that AWOL or desertion would cause them to receive a less-than-honorable discharge, which would make it difficult to get a good job. Unfortunately, "the concept of a lifelong stigma was too abstract to have any real meaning for them," according to Baskir and Strauss, who quote a battalion commander at Fort Meade: "The guy who had troubles usually had less intelligence and didn't think ahead. Most of these kids weren't bad. They were just dumb."[236] In 1975, the Presidential Clemency Board reviewed cases of Project 100,000 men who had gone AWOL and concluded that in some instances, the soldiers' mental limitations made it impossible for them to understand and obey rules and regulations.[237]

In a frequent scenario, a low-IQ man went AWOL because some of his buddies would persuade him to join them in running away. Left to his own devices, he might have lacked the skills to navigate from his unit into the outside world, but with comrades to help him, he could be successful.

Most men who went AWOL did not receive much publicity, but in one case, they attracted newspaper headlines. In 1968, the so-called Presidio Mutiny occurred at the Presidio stockade, a military prison in San Francisco. The stockade's 123 inmates were jammed together in an overcrowded building, which was supposed to hold only 88. Sometimes a man would have to wait two hours to go to one of the latrines, which were filthy and frequently backed up with excrement.

Almost all of the prisoners were AWOLs, and many of them were emotionally disturbed. There were numerous suicide attempts—some were real efforts, while others were gestures to appeal for psychiatric help or a discharge from the military. The guards responded by frequently beating the men or throwing them into "the hole" (solitary confinement).

On October 11, 1968, a prisoner named Richard "Rusty" Bunch, who was described by relatives as high-IQ but severely depressed and suicidal, asked a guard, "If I run, will you shoot me?" He requested that the guard aim at his head, and then he skipped away. He had gone only 30 feet when the guard killed him with a 12-gauge shotgun blast in his back.

The killing sparked a peaceful sit-down protest by 27 of the prisoners. Their spokesman tried to read a list of their grievances, but the prison commander, a 25-year-old captain, called in 75 MPs to encircle the huddled men and order a halt to the protest. When the men refused, all 27 were seized and charged with mutiny. The charge was later reduced to "willful disobedience of a lawful order." In the months following, three of the men escaped to Canada, two were found guilty of lesser charges, and the remaining 22 were found guilty, with sentences ranging from six months to 16 years. Ultimately, none of the men had to actually serve more than one year (thanks to the unfavorable publicity that the Army received).[238]

All 27 protesters were described by psychiatrists as misfits who had troubled backgrounds as well as emotional and intellectual deficits. "All of them," said Dr. Price Cobbs, a psychiatrist who examined them, "if given proper psychiatric testing by military authorities, would have been declared unfit for service."[239] At least five of the 27 were Project 100,000 men who were in the stockade because they had gone AWOL. Writer Peter Barnes describes one of them: "Danny Seals, from Auburn, California, was mildly retarded from a childhood brain injury. He had wanted to become a medic, but flunked the course at Fort Sam Houston and went AWOL in a fit of despondency. 'It was hard to learn in the Army,' he said."[240]

Writer Robert Sherrill described another soldier: Richard Stevens, 19, had an IQ of 66. He married his wife when she was 15 and pregnant. After he entered the Army, he went AWOL 15 times in one year. The psychiatrist who tested him observed that when he tried to do the simplest math problems, "he quickly became confused and his replies became so jumbled that one could not tell whether he was attempting to subtract, add, or was merely stating numbers at random."[241]

Writer Fred Gardner described a third prisoner: Billy Hayes, the son of a retired logger, was drafted in 1965 but was discovered to be unfit because of his low IQ. He was discharged, but the next year, when mental standards were lowered under Project 100,000, he was drafted again. He went AWOL three times from Fort Lewis and was sent to the stockade, where he tried to kill himself by drinking a bottle of Head & Shoulders shampoo. He spent several days in a hospital, where a physician explained to him that shampoo "will only cause diarrhea. It won't kill you."[242]

# 39

# Bad Paper

When it was time for Project 100,000 men to leave the military, many of them received a heavy blow. Slightly over half of them—180,000—were separated with discharges "under conditions other than honorable," a stigma that made it hard to get good jobs because many employers would not hire veterans who failed to produce a certificate of honorable discharge. They were often barred from veterans' benefits such as health care, housing assistance, and employment counseling. Some of them became chronically homeless and troubled.[243]

Although some "bad-paper" vets had been guilty of serious offenses, most had been accused of minor offenses related to the stresses of military life and combat: AWOL, missing duty, abusing alcohol or drugs, or talking back to a superior. Attorney David Addlestone, director of the National Veterans Law Center, said that one of the leading reasons that the military gave for bad-paper discharges for Project 100,000 men was "unsuitability."[244] This should be no surprise because many of the men were obviously unsuitable to be drafted in the first place. How perverse can you get? An unsuitable man is taken into the military and then returned to society—with stigma— for being unsuitable.

Baskir and Strauss tell of Gus Peters, who "came from a broken home, dropped out of school after the eighth grade, and was unemployed for most of his teenage years. His IQ was only 62.... His physical condition was no better." Drafted under Project 100,000, he was ridiculed by other soldiers, and he failed basic training. Unable to cope with military life, he went AWOL and was eventually given an undesirable discharge. When he left the service, "Peters was worse off than before. He still had no skills and no useful job experience, and he now was officially branded a misfit."[245]

There was a cruel irony in the less-than-honorable discharges. Millions of men who beat the draft legally (going to college, etc.) suffered nothing. In fact, they held an advantage over men who served: they got first crack at jobs and compiled seniority and experience. Even the draft-dodgers who fled to Canada and Sweden got an amnesty from Presidents Ford and Carter. But not McNamara's bad-paper vets. Unlike the articulate, politically astute war resisters, they had no one to lobby for them.

No one except a few heroes like Bill Daniel of Nashville, Tennessee, who had been an Army recruiter in 1967. When he was interviewed 35 years later, he was still bitter about the approximately 100 "McNamara's Morons" he had personally recruited in the slums of Cleveland, Ohio, during the war. "It didn't really sit too good with me," he said. "But when you are told what to do in the military, you do what you are told to do. They never should have been in the military..." Many of the low-aptitude men that he and his fellow recruiters signed up were either killed in combat or, when they left the Army, they departed with less-than-honorable discharges for such offenses as going AWOL, insubordination, and enuresis (bed-wetting). "You take a man who can't read or write," he said. "He never knew about deferments. He comes from the ghetto and he may not want to take orders, then you send him by the most expedient means necessary into combat. That's only going to lead to failure." In 2002, at the age of 71, he told a Nashville newspaper reporter that he had been devoting his life after the Army to petitioning the military to overturn the bad-paper discharges of McNamara's Morons. At that time, he had been successful in about 400 appeals.[246]

John Cook, a Collin County, Texas, Veterans Service Officer, said he was able to get benefits for several Project 100,000 men by using the argument that "they never should have been in the military." He told of one man who was accepted for military service despite being blind in one eye. "The attitude was, 'We can find something for them to do—just get them in the service.'"[247]

In the early 1980s, I got to know Jed Sluder (not his real name), a young man with an IQ of 68 who had been brought into the Navy under Project 100,000. He never went to Vietnam, but when his ship sailed into an American port, he often went AWOL and returned to his home in the Appalachian Mountains because of constant harassment by his shipmates. For example, some men would take him to the boiler room, strip off all his clothes, and rub grease all over him. Because of his AWOLs, the Navy gave him an undesirable discharge, a handicap which he made worse when he showed his discharge document to prospective employers, not realizing that it was a stigma. At home, his brothers taunted him for not completing his Navy service. One day—despite all he had been through— he tried to enlist in the Marine Corps, partly because he needed a job, partly because he wanted to prove to his brothers that "I'm a real man." The Marines, of course, turned him down because of his undesirable discharge.

I spent several months trying to persuade the Navy to change his discharge from undesirable to "general" so that he could qualify for veterans' educational and employment help. In the end, the uniformed officers on the Board for Correction of Naval Records, who were sympathetic to Project 100,000 veterans, voted unanimously in Sluder's favor, but they were overruled by an Assistant Secretary of the Navy, who was a political appointee (of President Ronald Reagan) with no U.S. Navy experience and no experience with Project 100,000 men.

Several veterans' counselors in the 1980s told me of similar experiences with low-IQ Vietnam veterans. When review boards were asked to change a discharge from undesirable to general, the uniformed officers (who were compassionate toward Project 100,000 men) would vote to approve the change, but they would be overruled by civilian superiors who regarded men who had gone AWOL as slackers who deserved no mercy. In an absurd turn of events, some of these civilians—who viewed themselves as "upholding military tradition"—had been draft avoiders during the Vietnam War. It was infuriating to see these officials kick the very men who had served in their stead.

# 40

# The Verdict on McNamara's Folly

At the dawn of Project 100,000, Robert McNamara boasted that the program would "salvage the poverty-scarred youth of our society at the rate of 100,000 men each year—first for two years of military service, and then for a lifetime of productive activity in civilian society."[248]

Despite the soaring optimism, Project 100,000 became known as "McNamara's Folly." By most measures, it was a failure, bringing more suffering than redemption. Charles Moskos, professor of sociology at Northwestern University and a specialist on American enlisted men, told me that "most of the career officers with whom I talk thought that Project 100,000 was ill-conceived and a fiasco.... It was a way of getting more bodies into the military under the rubric of welfare."[249]

Project 100,000 was advertised as "a great social experiment," said Jim Lane, a captain in the U.S. Army's Judge Advocate General's Corps. "It would give the Army troops, and in turn the Army would teach them to read and write and brush their teeth. But they never got around to teaching them anything. They just shipped them out to Vietnam."[250]

Though some Project 100,000 men did well in the service—passing basic training and going on to productive military assignments—large numbers of them had trouble coping with the demands of military life. They were often hazed and ridiculed and demeaned. (It was ironic that McNamara, in one of his speeches extolling Project 100,000, said, "I have directed that these men shall never be singled out or stigmatized in any manner."[251] Somehow his order never worked its way down to the company level.)

In announcing his program, McNamara never spoke of the possibility of death and injury. Even after the war, he never publicly acknowledged the thousands of Project 100,000 men who were killed and the tens of thousands who were wounded. But veterans remembered, and families remembered. In contemplating the names on the Vietnam Veterans Memorial Wall in Washington, DC, William F. Abbott, a Vietnam veteran, says, "John Kennedy said that life is unfair. True enough, but many of the surviving Vietnam casualty families would reply that the ultimate unfairness is death at an early age, in a land far from home, for reasons not clearly defined."[252] In response to this observation, another veteran noted that most of the men who avoided Vietnam were destined to die of old age, "while some large number of McNamara's 100,000 with room-temp IQs let into the Army in their stead" were slaughtered at a young age "in rice paddies half a world away."[253]

Some veterans of Project 100,000 were psychologically devastated by the war. Dr. John Wilson, a psychologist at Cleveland State University, who spent several years studying Vietnam veterans' emotional problems, estimated that thousands of Project 100,000 men who had served in Southeast Asia were so "severely messed up" that they couldn't function in society. "When I say 'severely messed up,' I mean they can't hold jobs, raise families, and cope with day-to-day living."[254]

McNamara had predicted that after they returned to civilian life, Project 100,000 men would have an earning capacity "two to three times what it would have been if there had been no such program."[255] After the war, however, a follow-up study on Project 100,000 men showed that in the 1986-1987 labor market, they were "either no better off or actually worse off" than non-veterans of similar aptitude.[256] So much for McNamara's rosy prediction.

In 2014, when many Vietnam veterans were entering their retirement years, a study funded by the Department of Veterans Affairs estimated that more than 283,000 veterans still suffered from post-traumatic stress disorder (PTSD), which was characterized by disabling flashbacks, hyper-arousal, and sleep problems. "The study's key takeaway is that for some, PTSD is not going away," said William Schlenger, a lead scientist on the study. "It is chronic and prolonged. For veterans with PTSD, the war is not over." The study found that low-IQ veterans were more likely to suffer from PTSD than high-IQ vets.[257]

Project 100,000 and McNamara's other failures in the war wrecked his reputation. "At first admired for his intelligence and analytical prowess," author Thomas Sticht wrote, McNamara "later became one of the most hated men in America by the officers and enlisted personnel he had led."[258] One officer, angry over the abuse of mentally limited men in the Armed Forces, even confronted McNamara in public. At a conference in Washington, DC, as McNamara touted the virtues of Project 100,000, an Army psychologist who was treating psychologically afflicted Vietnam veterans at Walter Reed Army Medical Center stood up and spoke out. Although he was a "mere" captain, Dr. Walter P. Knake told McNamara, "What you are doing is wrong!"[259]

Some military men were most enraged by the criminals and misfits that were brought into the Armed Forces. Marine Corps veteran John W. Geymann said he ended his service in 1970 primarily because of the chaos and lack of discipline caused by "thugs" who were admitted with criminal-record waivers. "Thefts, strong-armed robberies, assaults, and an almost ubiquitous drug culture permeated the fiber of our Corps," he said. "Given the opportunity to choose, who would knowingly opt to serve in garrison or in combat alongside a substandard record-waivered enlistee?"[260]

Did McNamara ever express regret over Project 100,000? Biographer Deborah Shapley says that to the very end, he refused to apologize or admit error. He was resentful of the term "McNamara's Moron Corps," which he had heard for years, and he steadfastly believed that the program was beneficial to individual men and to society in general.[261] He must have used selective vision, ignoring the many accounts of abuse, suffering, and death, while looking only at success stories about some Project 100,000 men who did well in the service. McNamara told Shapley of an incident that occurred after he left the Pentagon and became president of the World Bank. "As he debarked from a plane, a black soldier standing at attention saluted. Beneath his cap the man beamed a wide grin.... 'Proud to meet you, sir,' said the man, still at attention and smiling. 'I'm one of your morons.' McNamara pumped the man's hand gleefully.... He rushed off still laughing at this brief moment of appreciation."[262]

McNamara wanted to believe that Project 100,000 was a universally successful program, but his self-congratulation was at odds with the verdict of most scholars and other observers. Historian Christian G. Appy said Project 100,000 "was instituted with high-minded rhetoric about offering the poor an opportunity to serve. Its result, however, was to send many poor, terribly confused, and woefully undereducated boys to risk death in Vietnam."[263] Anni P. Baker, a history professor at Wheaton College in Norton, Massachusetts, said that "Project 100,000, or 'McNamara's Morons,' as the cruel joke went, was a disaster, benefitting neither the men nor the Armed Forces."[264] Jacob Heilbrunn of Georgetown University said that "McNamara's experiment in social engineering had the most awful results," including ridicule in training camps and death in Vietnam.[265] Samuel F. Yette, a professor at Howard University, said that instead of preparing impoverished young men with skills for a better life, Project 100,000 was "little more than an express vehicle to Vietnam."[266]

Denouncing McNamara for his "intellectual arrogance and duplicity," Myra MacPherson, author of the Vietnam classic *Long Time Passing*, called Project 100,000 "a shameful brainchild" and "one of his most heinous acts as the chief architect of the war."[267]

Lawrence M. Baskir and William A. Strauss, who were senior officials on President Ford's Clemency Board, summarized the major failings of Project 100,000: "It was a failure for the recruits themselves. They never got the training that military service seemed to promise. They were the last to be promoted and the first to be sent to Vietnam. They saw more than their share of combat and got more than their share of bad discharges. Many ended up with greater difficulties in civilian society than when they started. For them, it was an ironic and tragic conclusion to a program that promised special treatment and a brighter future, and denied both."[268]

# 41

# The Folly Continues

O n the last day of 1971, Project 100,000 was officially ended, and in July, 1973, the draft was replaced by the All-Volunteer Force (AVF). The passing score on the AFQT was raised from 10th percentile (IQ of 72) to the old standard of 31st percentile (IQ of 92).

The end of Project 100,000 did not mean, however, that the services stopped accepting recruits of low intelligence. The Army and Marine Corps were given permission—whenever they failed to meet monthly recruiting quotas—to enlist recruits who had scored in Category IV (between 10th and 31st percentiles). Both branches tried to avoid taking these individuals, but sometimes they had to induct them in order to fill the ranks.[269]

In 1976, a congressman from Texas, Charles Wilson, testified at a hearing about the death of one of his constituents, Lynn McClure, who "was a 20-year-old young man from Lufkin, Texas, who had a history of nonsuccess, who was mentally retarded, who weighed 115 pounds. He somehow got into the Marine Corps, and was severely beaten during basic training and died as a result of those injuries without regaining consciousness."[270]

In Tulsa, Oklahoma, in 1976, a 25-year-old man walked out of a state mental institution, where he had lived for 14 years, and wandered into an Army recruiting station. He had been diagnosed as having what today is called Down syndrome, and he was labeled as "severely retarded." When he entered the recruiting station, he was promptly enlisted by a sergeant who (a later investigation revealed) faked his test scores. He was sent to Fort Ord, California, for basic training, but he soon deserted and came back to Tulsa. He was arrested and put in the Fort Sill stockade to face court-martial. When the Oklahoma Association for Retarded Citizens discovered that a severely retarded man was facing court-martial for desertion, it retained a lawyer and sent hundreds of angry letters to Washington. This caused the Army to back off, and it announced that it would give the man a discharge. But when it turned out to be a *dishonorable* discharge, the ARC members again raised an outcry, and with the assistance of Congressman James R. Jones, they succeeded in getting the Army to simply void the enlistment. Why did the man join the Army? A psychiatrist who examined him found that he had the mental capacity of a nine-year-old child. His enlistment "probably reflects his need to belong and gain security, along with the wonder and interest in being a soldier appropriate to a nine-year-old child."[271]

In 1980, at Fort Benning, a reporter quoted a member of the military police: "I've had people come up to me and say, 'How do I get back to my unit?' I ask, 'What's your unit?' And then they answer that they don't know. So I ask them what their orders say. They reply, 'I can't read my orders. All I know is that my unit is in a big, white building.'"[272]

In the drawn-out wars in Iraq and Afghanistan, beginning in 2001, the U.S. did not bring back the draft, but there were many parallels to Vietnam, as the military accepted low-performing recruits because it was desperate for more and more soldiers for combat. In 2008, an Army private named David Dietrich of Perry County, Pennsylvania, was the subject of a *Newsweek* article entitled "He Should Never Have Gone to Iraq." Before and during his Army time, he was considered slow in his thinking, and he had trouble retaining information. In basic training, he couldn't hit targets on the rifle range, even though he was given extra training. One superior campaigned to have Dietrich sent home on grounds that he would pose a danger to himself and others if he was sent to Iraq, but the request was rebuffed by higher-ups. As with Vietnam, there was a big push to get troops into the combat zone. Soon after he arrived in Iraq, he was assigned to act as a scout in an abandoned building, where he was supposed to watch furtively from open windows. A few minutes after he started his duty at one of the windows, he was shot dead.[273]

As with Vietnam, recruiters for Iraq and Afghanistan were under great pressure to fill quotas. In 2006, during an intense phase of the Iraq war when the military was desperate for fresh troops, ABC News sent undercover students with hidden video cameras into 10 recruiting stations in New York, New Jersey, and Connecticut. The six-month investigation revealed that "recruiters will say anything" to get young people to sign up, according to ABC News. When one student asked, "Will I be going to war?" a recruiter answered, "I would say your chances will be slim to none." When a different recruiter was asked if anyone was being sent to Iraq, he replied, "No, we're bringing people back." Another recruiter told a student that if he didn't like the Army, he could simply quit. One student posed as a drug addict, and the recruiter offered to help him cheat to get into the Army. A woman named Sue Niederer, whose son Seth was killed in Iraq, told ABC that recruiters had promised her son that he would not see combat.[274]

In 2007, nine Marine Corps recruiters who worked in the Houston area were punished for using stand-ins to take the mental tests at the Houston induction center for 15 "marginal" prospects who might not have passed on their own. The fraud was caught by an official who noticed that the signatures of test takers didn't match those on enlistment forms. No one knew how long fraudulent test-taking had been going on.[275]

During the wars in Iraq and Afghanistan, the military repeated one of the worst mistakes of the Vietnam War by accepting inductees who had committed crimes as civilians. From 2004 through 2007, the four major branches of the Armed Forces granted 125,000 "moral waivers" to override the rule against accepting people with criminal records. Many of the waivers were for minor offenses such as drunk and disorderly conduct, but some were for serious crimes such as aggravated assault, burglary, robbery, and vehicular homicide.[276] Some of the ex-offenders performed well in Iraq and Afghanistan, but some wreaked harm. The most notorious offender was Private Steven Green, 20, an angry misfit and high-school dropout from Midland, Texas, who had racked up jail time for drug and alcohol offenses before he joined the Army with a moral waiver. In 2006, Green and four other soldiers in Iraq drank alcohol, changed into black clothes, and then raided the home of a husband and wife and their two daughters. Green killed the parents and the younger daughter. Then he and a second soldier raped the 14-year-old daughter, shot her, and set fire to her body to try to destroy evidence.[277] He was convicted of rape and murder, and sentenced to life in prison. In 2014, he committed suicide by hanging himself in his cell at the federal maximum security prison in Tucson, Arizona.[278]

In 2007, a senior NCO involved in personnel and recruiting said that the Army had lowered standards to accept law violations that were worse than previously permitted and to allow test scores that were lower than previously accepted. "We're really scraping the bottom of the barrel to get people to join," he said.[279]

In 2009, a 20-year-old man with autism and a low IQ was picked up by a Marine recruiter at an Irvine, California, group home for the mentally disabled and driven to a recruitment center to sign up for the Marine Corps. Once in boot camp, according to the *Los Angeles Times*, "he was confused by the orders drill instructors shouted at him. He was caught stealing peanut butter from the chow hall. He urinated in his canteen. He talked back to the drill instructors. He refused to shave." He was eventually discharged from the Marines.[280]

In the era of Middle East wars, Project 100,000 was long gone, but the memory lingered. Writing in 2009, Michael Broihier said that in the Marine Corps "you'd occasionally hear an older officer or NCO refer to a particularly knuckleheaded Marine as one of 'McNamara's 100,000.' I knew what they meant; the Marine in question was probably a danger to himself and those around him."[281]

# Epilogue

One of the lessons of McNamara's Project 100,000 is that low-aptitude individuals should never be used in a war zone or in dangerous rear-echelon areas. Putting their lives at risk is cruel and immoral, and on a sheer practical level, it degrades the effectiveness of war efforts.

The least intelligent among us should never be viewed as expendable units of manpower, but as our fellow sojourners on this fragile earth, deserving respect and compassion—and gratitude for the contributions they make to our families and to our society.

While vowing to never again induct people with intellectual disabilities, Americans should also heed warnings by military leaders that it is a mistake to take in inductees who have criminal backgrounds, medical defects, social maladjustment, and psychiatric disorders. The Armed Forces need—and deserve—the best and the brightest.

One of the wisest quotations that I recorded earlier in this book comes from Lieutenant Colonel Leslie John Shellhase, a World War II veteran who helped create Project 100,000 but was strongly opposed to sending the men into combat: "Wars are not won by using marginal manpower as cannon fodder, but rather by risking, and sometimes losing, the flower of a nation's youth."

# Appendix

# Samples from the AFQT

The AFQT (Armed Forces Qualification Test) had 100 multiple-choice questions, and one hour was allowed. The questions started out easy and got progressively harder. Here are some sample questions from Defense Department brochures that were given to potential servicemen in the 1960s to help them understand how the test worked.

## 1. Arithmetic Reasoning

An example of an easy question:

1. 7 + 14 =
   A. 21
   B. 22
   C. 23
   D. 24

Examples of more difficult questions:

2. A boy buys a sandwich for 20 cents, milk for 10 cents, and pie for 15 cents. How much does he pay for all?
   A. 30 cents
   B. 35 cents
   C. 45 cents
   D. 50 cents

3. Twenty men contribute $25 each for a Christmas party. Forty per cent of the money is spent for food and drinks. How much is left for other expenses?
    A. $125
    B. $200
    C. $300
    D. $375

## 2.   Word Knowledge

An example of an easy question:

4. A <u>rose</u> is a kind of:
    A. animal
    B. bird
    C. fish
    D. flower

Examples of more difficult questions:

5. <u>Awkward</u> most nearly means:
    A. ignorant
    B. dangerous
    C. clumsy
    D. vulgar

6. <u>Irate</u> most nearly means:
    A. irresponsible
    B. insubordinate
    C. untidy
    D. angry

## 3.   Mechanical Comprehension

7. Which upright supports the greater part of the load?

A. upright A
B. upright B
C. They support it equally
D. It cannot be determined

8. Which bridge is the strongest?

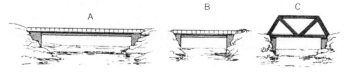

A. A
B. B
C. C
D. All are equally strong

9. At which point was the basketball moving slowest?

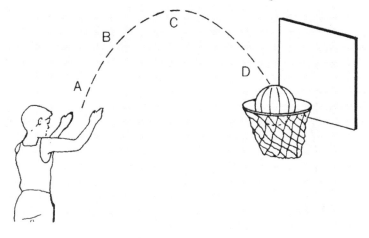

A. A
B. B
C. C
D. D

## 4.  Space Perception

10. Which box could this pattern make?

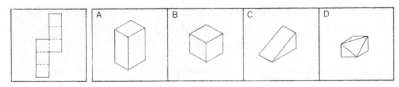

11. Which of the four patterns would result when the box is unfolded?

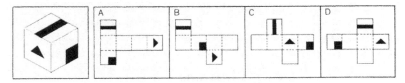

## Answers

1. A
2. C
3. C
4. D
5. C
6. D
7. A
8. C
9. C
10. B
11. D

# Acknowledgements

S pecial thanks to my wife Merrell for shoring up my resolve over the years by reminding me of her belief that I was probably the only man in America who had the experiences and the commitment to tell the whole story of McNamara's Folly— "a story that needs to be told." And a note of appreciation to my old Army buddy George A. Frazier of Marin County, California, who listened to my accounts of Fort Benning events a few months after they occurred and encouraged me to write them down.

I am also indebted to the following men and women, who provided me with information, encouragement, or inspiration: David Addlestone, Ron Bitzer, Bob Bowles, Jim Bracewell, George Buford, Jan Caldwell, Walt and Carole Currie, Nicholas B. Deane, Frank J. Edwards, M.D., Artie Egendorf, Major Ronald J. Ellefson, James Fallows, Merrell and John Foote, Lieutenant Colonel Alvin E. Fort, Joseph L. Galloway, David F. Godshalk, Rolfe Godshalk, Colonel David Hackworth, Richard L. Hatch, Melody Hays, Brigadier General Hugh B. Hester, David Holcombe, Inette Miller 'Īmaikalani, 'Iokepa Hanalei 'Īmaikalani, Myra MacPherson, Kate Mathews, Celia Miles, Ruth Ann and Malcolm Miller-Jones, Charles Moskos, June Newton, Keith William Nolan, Jim and Rolfe Olsen, Wallace and Susan Paterson, Chief Hospital Corpsman Don Phelps, Barry Romo, Lieutenant Colonel Leslie John Shellhase, James E. Westheider, and Don Winter.

# Illustration Credits

p. 47, Figure 1. Marine recruits: Courtesy of the U.S. Department of Defense. Photo by Lance Cpl. Bridget M. Keane, U.S. Marine Corps.

p. 48, Figure 2. Navy SEAL: Courtesy of the U.S. Navy. Photo by Mass Communication Specialist 2nd Class Marcos T. Hernandez.

pp. 53-61, Figures 3 - 7. Photos taken by the author in 1972 at a PT test for soldiers at Fort Bliss, Texas.

p. 74, Figure 8. Obstacle Course: Courtesy of U.S. Air Force. Photo by Senior Airman Dan Gage.

pp. 215-216: All of the illustrations in the Appendix are courtesy of the Defense Department, which used them in brochures in the 1960s to help potential servicemembers to understand the AFQT.

# Sources

M ost of the observations and dialogue at Fort Benning came from my memory and from letters that I wrote to my fiancée (later my wife) Merrell in the summer of 1967 shortly after events occurred. My research on Project 100,000 was begun in the 1970s and was carried on sporadically for the next four and a half decades. Some of the anecdotes about McNamara's Boys were supplied by veterans whom I interviewed over the years at Veterans Affairs hospitals. Other stories came from veterans' recollections in blogs, articles, and books.

1    Major Joseph B. Berger III, "Making Little Rocks Out of Big Rocks: Implementing Sentences to Hard Labor Without Confinement," *The Army Lawyer*, Department of the Army Pamphlet 27-50-379, December 2004, pp. 1-17.

2    Myra C. Glenn, *Jack Tar's Story: The Autobiographies and Memoirs of Sailors in Antebellum America* (Cambridge: Cambridge University Press, 2010), pp. 54-56; Keith Mercer, "Northern Exposure: Resistance to Naval Impressment in British North America, 1775-1815," *The Canadian Historical Review*, June 2010, pp. 199-232; Markus Eder, *Crime and Punishment in the Royal Navy of the Seven Years' War, 1755-1763* (Aldershot, England: Ashgate Publishing, 2004), pp. 31-33.

3    Alfred A. Cave, *The French and Indian War* (Westport, CT: Greenwood, 2004), p. 89.

4    Amanda Foreman, "America on Fire," *Smithsonian*, July-August 2014, p. 39.

5   Lisa Hsiao, "Project 100,000: The Great Society's Answer to Military Manpower Needs in Vietnam," *Vietnam Generation*, Spring 1989, p. 17.

6   "Women in the Vietnam War," *History*, www.history.com, accessed March 23, 2014.

7   "American Civilian and Military Women Who Died in the Vietnam War," *The Virtual Wall*, www.virtualwall.org, accessed March 23, 2014.

8   Clark Dougan, Samuel Lipsman, and the editors of Boston Publishing Co., *A Nation Divided* (Boston: Boston Publishing Company, 1984), p. 76.

9   "Military Records," National Archives, archives.gov/research/military, accessed January 23, 2014.

10   Tom Clancy and General Tony Zinni, *Battle Ready* (New York: Berkley Books, 2004), p. 118.

11   Lawrence M. Baskir and William A. Strauss, *Chance and Circumstance: The Draft, the War, and the Vietnam Generation* (New York: Alfred A. Knopf, 1978), p. 29.

12   James Ebert, *A Life in a Year: The American Infantryman in Vietnam* (New York: Random House/Presidio Press, 2007), p. 446.

13   Baskir and Strauss, p. 33.

14   Baskir and Strauss, pp. 30-33.

15   The fatherhood deferment was available from 1963 to 1970. It was ended April 23, 1970, by President Richard Nixon.

16   "James Fallows on the Draft," *Washington Monthly*, November 2009, washingtonmonthly.com, accessed March 14, 2014.

17   Charles Kaiser, *1968 in America* (New York: Grove Press, 1988), p. 120.

18   Christian G. Appy, *Working-Class War: American Combat Soldiers & Vietnam* (Chapel Hill: University of North Carolina Press, 1993), p. 33.

19   Clark Dougan, and others, pp. 77-78.

20   "Bill Clinton's Vietnam Test," editorial, *The New York Times*, published February 14, 1992, and retrieved from www.nytimes.com, January 28, 2014.

21   Baskir and Strauss, pp. 44-45.

22   Baskir and Strauss, pp. 48-49.

23 James E. Westheider (professor of history, University of Cincinnati—Clermont College), *The Vietnam War* (Westport, CT: Greenwood Press, 2007), p. 38.

24 Julie Ross, "Honor the Vietnam War's Conscientious Objectors," *ForceChange*, forcechange.com, Sept. 1, 2013.

25 John Lithgow, *Drama: An Actor's Education* (New York: HarperCollins, 2011), pp. 170-172.

26 Mark Helprin, "I Dodged the Draft and I Was Wrong," transcript of a speech delivered at West Point, October 11, 1992. Reprinted in *National Review Archives*, old.nationalreview.com, accessed February 15, 2014.

27 Joan Didion, "Cheney: The Fatal Touch," *The New York Review*, Oct. 5, 2006, p. 55.

28 Paul Marx, "Reconsider the Draft," *Baltimore Sun*, baltimoresun.com, May 24, 2010.

29 Ebert, p. 20.

30 Alan Vanneman, "A Veteran's Outrage," *The Charlotte Observer*, January 4, 1984, p. 11A.

31 Westheider, pp. 35-36.

32 Westheider, pp. 31-34.

33 Maury Maverick Jr., quoted by *Texas Observer*, Oct. 6, 1978, p. 18.

34 Geoffrey Kabaservice, *The Guardians* (New York: Macmillan, 2005), p. 290.

35 Congressman Charles Wilson, in *Hearings on Marine Corps' Recruit Training and Recruiting Programs,* Subcommittee on Military Personnel of the Committee on Armed Services, House of Representatives (Washington: U.S. Government Printing Office, 1976), p. 4.

36 Bernard Rostker, *I Want You!: The Evolution of the All-Volunteer Force* (Santa Monica, CA: RAND Corporation, 2006), p. 136; Homer Bigart, "McNamara Plans to 'Salvage' 40,000 Rejected in Draft," *New York Times*, August 24, 1966, p. 1.

37 Robert S. McNamara, *The Essence of Security* (New York: Harper & Row, 1968), p. 134.

38 Kaiser, p. 96; Kenneth Cukier and Viktor Mayer-Schönberger, "The Dictatorship of Data," *MIT Technology Review*, technologyreview.com, posted May 31, 2013.

[39] Deborah Shapley, *Promise and Power: The Life and Times of Robert McNamara* (Boston: Little, Brown and Company, 1993), p. 204.

[40] Paul Starr, *The Discarded Army: Veterans after Vietnam* (New York: Charterhouse, 1973), pp. 186-188.

[41] Transcript of a conversation between President Lyndon Johnson and Secretary Robert McNamara on November 14, 1964, as secretly recorded on White House tapes, Michael R. Beschloss (editor), *Reaching for Glory: Lyndon Johnson's Secret White House Tapes, 1964-1965* (New York: Simon & Schuster, 2002), pp. 140-141.

[42] Transcript, pp. 140-141.

[43] Department of the Army, *Marginal Men and Military Service* (Washington: Department of the Army, 1965), p. 34; Edward J. Drea, *McNamara, Clifford, and the Burdens of Vietnam 1965-1969* (Washington, DC: Historical Office, Office of the Secretary of Defense, 2011), p. 266.

[44] Rand Corporation, *Project 100,000 New Standards Program*, monograph posted online, www.rand.org, accessed February 23, 2014.

[45] Testimony of Dr. Wayne S. Sellman, Director for Accession Policy, Office of the Assistant Secretary of Defense (Force Management and Personnel), "Post-service Experiences of Project 100,000 Veterans," Hearings before the Subcommittee on Oversight and Investigations, House Committee on Veterans Affairs, February 28, 1990, pp. 3-15.

[46] Peter Barnes, *Pawns: The Plight of the Citizen-Soldier* (New York: Alfred A. Knopf, 1972), p. 37.

[47] The sample test questions appeared in an Armed Forces booklet distributed to potential recruits in the 1960s.

[48] A.J. Martin, Director, Accession Policy, "Relationship between AFQT and IQ," memo from the Office of the Secretary of Defense, Sept. 4, 1980, p. 3.

[49] Beth L. Bailey, *America's Army: Making the All-Volunteer Force* (Cambridge, MA: Belknap Press of Harvard University Press, 2009), pp. 98-99; Robert K. Griffith Jr., *The U.S. Army's Transition to the All-Volunteer Force, 1968-1974* (Washington, DC: Center of Military History, United States Army, 1997), p. 187; Richard

Homan, "Low-IQ Recruit Plan Stirs Complaints," *Washington Post*, June 29, 1969, p. G1.

50 Don Winter, "Drafted in Spite of the Score," a sidebar to "Project 100,000—The Forgotten Men of the War." *National Journal*, April 15, 1978, p. 589.

51 George Buford, *Draft Dodging* (Bloomington, IN: Xlibris, 2007), p. 47; Military Entrance Processing Station (MEPS), *Army Regulation 601-270*, www.apd.army.mil. Posted April 4, 2007.

52 Jamie Kelso, quoted by Michael Medved and David Wallechinsky, *What Really Happened to the Class of '65?* (New York: Random House, 1976), pp. 198-199.

53 "Military Personnel Data Files and Reporting Procedures for Project One Hundred Thousand," *Department of Defense Instruction 1145.3*, November 29, 1967.

54 David Robinson, GI and veterans' counselor in Houston, Texas, in the late 1960s, telephone interview with the author, October 8, 1978.

55 Don Winter, letter to the author, August 16, 1978.

56 Robinson.

57 Winter, "Drafted in Spite of the Score," p. 589.

58 Beth J. Asch, and others, *Military Enlistment of Hispanic Youth: Obstacles and Opportunities* (Arlington, VA: RAND National Defense Research Institute, 2009), p. 93.

59 United States Senate Committee on Veterans' Affairs, *Hearings, Reports and Prints of the Senate Committee on Veterans' Affairs* (Washington: U.S. Government Printing Office, 1977), p. 750.

60 G. David Curry, *Sunshine Patriots: Punishment and the Vietnam Offender* (South Bend, IN: University of Notre Dame Press, 1985), p. 137.

61 Buford, pp. 47-48.

62 Lea Ybarra, *Vietnam Veteranos: Chicanos Recall the War* (Austin: University of Texas Press, 2004), pp. 52-53.

63 George M. Watson, Jr., *Voices from the Rear: Vietnam 1969-1970* (Bloomington, IN: Xlibris, 2001), p. 25.

64 Myra MacPherson, *Long Time Passing: Vietnam & the Haunted Generation* (New York: Doubleday, 1984), p. 642.

65 Barnes, pp. 33-45.

66    MacPherson, p. 642.

67    "Military Recruiting Practices," Hearings before the Subcommittee on Manpower and Personnel of the Committee on Armed Services, United States Senate (October 10 and 12, 1978), p. 47. (Although the hearings took place after the end of Project 100,000, they dealt with misconduct that happened during the Project 100,000 years.)

68    "Marine Corps' Recruit Training and Recruiting Programs," Hearings before the Subcommittee on Military Personnel of the Committee on Armed Services, U.S. House of Representatives (May 24-August 9, 1976), pp. 81-115. (Although the hearings took place after the end of Project 100,000, they dealt with misconduct that happened during the Project 100,000 years.)

69    Terry Hughes, personal interview, October 3, 1979.

70    Mark Lloyd, *Dragon Chaser: A Memoir* (Bloomington, IN: iUniverse, 2013), p. 7.

71    Larry Heinemann, *Black Virgin Mountain: A Return to Vietnam* (New York: Knopf Doubleday, 2005), p. 12.

72    Westheider, p. 56.

73    Kyle Longley, *Grunts: The American Combat Soldier in Vietnam* (Armonk, NY: M.E. Sharpe, 2008), p. 8.

74    Baskir and Strauss, pp. 127-128.

75    Baskir and Strauss, p. 128.

76    Shapley, p. 385.

77    Appy, *Working-Class War*, p. 32.

78    Captain David Anthony Dawson, U.S. Marine Corps, "The Impact of Project 100,000 on the Marine Corps." Master of Arts thesis, Kansas State University, Manhattan, Kansas, 1994, p. 178.

79    Gregg Stoner, *The Yellow Footprints to Hell and Back* (New York: iUniverse, Inc., 2008), p. 97.

80    Starr, p. 194.

81    MacPherson, p. 642.

82    "Whatever Happened to Military Service for Youths Below 1-A?" *U.S. News & World Report*, Sept. 6, 1971, p. 56.

83    Malcolm Riley, former sergeant, U.S. Army, personal interview at Charles George VA Medical Center, Oteen, North Carolina, November 7, 1997.

84  Hughes, interview.

85  Winter, p. 590.

86  A Navy veteran who used the online name, ltn72@charter.net, "Mr. Rangel's Bitter Hypocrisy," *The Nav Log*, www.navlog.org, accessed March 14, 2014.

87  Lieutenant Colonel David Evans, U.S. Marine Corps, "Losing Battle," *The New Republic*, June 30, 1986, pp. 12-13.

88  I was given this sad statistic in the 1970s by a former insider at ODCSPER (Office of the Deputy Chief of Staff, Personnel), who viewed the use of Project 100,000 men in combat as a "shameful" perversion of the original intent to restrict low-IQ men to rear-area support roles. At the time, the Pentagon was providing a lower number, which my source said was misleading in that it counted only "killed in action" fatalities, omitting deaths from landmines, booby traps, accidents, and other causes. The 5,478 total includes men who died in any combat-related situation, those who died in training, those who were wounded and subsequently died in a military hospital in Vietnam, Japan, or the U.S., those who died in aircraft/helicopter incidents, those who were presumed dead (body remains not recovered), and those who died from noncombat causes (such as illness, accidents, murder, and suicide).

89  The estimate of the number wounded is based on A.T. Lawrence's statement that "3.7 soldiers were wounded for each [American] man killed in action" in Vietnam and there was a ratio of "one amputee for every 11 deaths." A.T. Lawrence, *Crucible Vietnam: Memoir of an Infantry Lieutenant* (Jefferson, NC: McFarland & Company, Publishers, 2009), p. 217.

90  Joseph L. Galloway, "100,000 Reasons to Shed No Tears for McNamara," published July 7, 2009, shortly after the death of Robert McNamara, McClatchy newspapers, mcclatchydc.com, accessed January 24, 2014.

91  David Hackworth, "Dumbing Down the Army," essay published Aug. 31, 1999, on www.wnd.com, accessed December 20, 2013.

92  Leslie John Shellhase, Lieutenant Colonel, U.S. Army (Retired) and a professor at the University of Alabama, letter to the author, July 12, 1978.

93  Paul D. Walker, *Jungle Dragoon: The Memoir of an Armored Cav Platoon Leader in Vietnam* (Novato, CA: Presidio Press, 1999), p. 94.

94  Charles Cooper, quoted by Christian Appy, *Patriots: The Vietnam War Remembered from All Sides* (New York: Penguin, 2004), p. 445.

95  Testimony of Congressman William Steiger in *Status of the All-Volunteer Armed Force*, transcript of a hearing before the Subcommittee on Manpower and Personnel of the Committee on Armed Services, United States Senate (June 20, 1978), p. 75.

96  General William Westmoreland, quoted by Samuel Hynes, *The Soldiers' Tale: Bearing Witness to a Modern War* (New York: Penguin, 1998), p. 183.

97  Arnold R. Isaacs, *Vietnam Shadows: The War, Its Ghosts, and Its Legacy* (Baltimore, MD: The Johns Hopkins University Press, 1997), p. 40.

98  Colonel Robert D. Heinl, Jr., "The Collapse of the Armed Forces," *Armed Forces Journal*, June 7, 1971, p. 7.

99  Richard A. Gabriel (with Paul L. Savage), *Crisis in Command: Mismanagement in the Army* (New York: Hill and Wang, 1979), p. 10.

100  Clancy and Zinni, p. 117.

101  James Webb, "The Draft: Why the Army Needs It," *The Atlantic*, April 1980, pp. 34-44.

102  William F. Walsh, "Can the Military Cope with Thirteen Books?" *American Bar Association Journal*, January 1964, pp. 66-68.

103  Lieutenant Colonel Charles L. Armstrong, U.S. Marine Corps, "Profile of a Small Unit Warrior," *Marine Corps Gazette*, April, 1990, pp. 19-20.

104  All of the information on the Romo family comes from these sources: Andrew Hunt, *The Turning: A History of Vietnam Veterans Against the War* (New York: New York University Press, 1999), p. 80; Interview with Barry L. Romo, April 7, 2001, "Experiencing War: Stories from the Veterans History Project," Library of Congress, lcweb2.loc.gov, accessed January 17, 2014; Mokneque Clark, Alison Paddock & Kwami Patterson, "Students, Scholars Debate Military Draft Reinstatement as Iraqi Conflict Heats Up," *The Columbia Chronicle*, columbiachronicle.com, posted Jan. 13,

2003; Barry Romo, "The Never Ending War," Vietnam Veterans Against the War, www.vvaw.org, accessed January 17, 2014.

[105] Lieutenant Colonel Robert Kimball, U.S. Army (Retired), *Guns, Books and Lawsuits: A Memoir* (Bloomington, IN: AuthorHouse, 2012), p. 93.

[106] Sergeant Major Francis T. McNeive, quoted by Dawson, pp. 124-125.

[107] Keith William Nolan, *House to House: Playing the Enemy's Game in Saigon, May 1968* (St. Paul, MN: Zenith Press, 2006), pp. 63, 274.

[108] Dawson, p. 135.

[109] Eliot Cohen, quoted by Beth L. Bailey, *America's Army: Making the All-Volunteer Force* (Cambridge, MA: Belknap Press of Harvard University Press, 2009), p. 107.

[110] BillT (Bill Tuttle, Chief Warrant Officer 4), on the military blog *Castle Argghhh!*, thedonovan.com/archives, posted July 7, 2009, accessed December 12, 2013.

[111] G.J. Lau, *SitRep Negative: A Year in Vietnam* (Frederick, MD: The Windroot Press, 2011), pp. 89-91.

[112] Ebert, pp. 157-158.

[113] Tim Page and John Timlott, *Nam: The Vietnam Experience, 1965-75* (New York: Barnes and Noble Books, 1995), p. 441.

[114] Robert Nylen, *Guts* (New York: Random House, 2009), pp. 14-16.

[115] Bill Peters, *First Force Recon Company: Sunrise at Midnight* (New York: Ballantine Books, 1999), pp. 137-138.

[116] Guenter Lewy, *America in Vietnam* (New York: Oxford University Press, 1978), p. 309. Lewy reported that 23.7 percent of U.S. deaths were caused by mines and booby traps. The estimate for Project 100,000 men was extrapolated by using the 23.7 figure.

[117] All of the information about Ward comes from John L. Ward, *Moron Corps: A Vietnam Veteran's Case for Action* (Houston: Strategic Book Publishing, 2012), pp. 1-71.

[118] Natalie M. Rosinsky, *The Draft Lottery* (North Mankato, MN: Compass Point Books, 2009), p. 16; Westheider, p. 42.

[119] Appy, *Working-Class War*, p. 37.

[120] Leslie Fiedler, "Who Really Died in Vietnam?" *Saturday Review*, December 1972, pp. 40-41.

[121] Margaret Malamud, *Ancient Rome and Modern America* (New York: John Wiley & Sons, 2009), pp. 48-49.

[122] Camillo "Mac" Bica, PhD (a Vietnam veteran and former Marine Corps officer), "Rich Man's War and a Poor Man's Fight," *Truthout*, truth-out.org, accessed January 22, 2014; "The New York City Anti-Draft Riots," *Answers*, answers.com, accessed January 22, 2014.

[123] Congressman William A. Steiger, quoted in Stuart H. Loory, *Defeated: Inside America's Military Machine* (New York: Random House, 1973), p. 193.

[124] Appy, *Working-Class War*, pp. 6-7.

[125] Marc Jason Gilbert, *The Vietnam War on Campus* (Westport, CT: Praeger, 2001), p. 221.

[126] Baskir and Strauss, p. 6.

[127] William Broyles, *Goodbye Vietnam* (New York: Open Road Media, 2013), p. 5.

[128] Nylen, pp. 70-72.

[129] Ebert, p. 148.

[130] Ronald J. Glasser, M.D., *365 Days* (New York: George Braziller, 1971), p. 91; Daniel E. Evans Jr. and Charles W. Sasser, *Doc: Platoon Medic* (Lincoln, NE: iUniverse, 2002), p. 202; Paul O'Connell, *Letters Home*, vietvet.org/pocindex.htm, accessed November 26, 2013; "The Final Mission," Newsletter of A Company, 2nd Battalion, 12th Infantry Regiment, Vietnam, 1966-67, alphaassociation.homestead.com, accessed November 26, 2013.

[131] Wayne Johnson, Vietnam veteran, personal interview at Charles George VA Medical Center, Oteen, North Carolina, November 12, 1997.

[132] Nolan, p. 323.

[133] Gary B. Roberts, interview, Kennesaw State University Oral History Project, January 31, 2005 and February 2, 2005, kennesaw.edu, accessed January 12, 2014.

[134] Sergeant Gerry Barker, quoted by James R. Ebert, *A Life in a Year: The American Infantryman in Vietnam* (New York: Ballantine Books/Presidio Press, 1993), p. 155.

[135] Broyles, p. 10.

[136] Evans and Sasser, pp. 71-93.

[137] Buford, pp. 18-19.

[138] Gregory D. Foster, "A Veteran's View of Bush and War," *Christian Science Monitor*, csmonitor.com, accessed February 8, 2014.

[139] Lewis B. Puller, Jr, *Fortunate Son: The Autobiography of Lewis B. Puller, Jr.* (New York: Bantam, 1993), pp. 90-91.

[140] Dr. Lawrence William, *The Broken Man*, a book posted online, williamblogstuff.blogspot.com, accessed January 7, 2014.

[141] Dr. William.

[142] H. Michael Sweeney, "Can You Outrun a Nuclear Missile?" Cosmopark, cosmopark.ru/rascal.html, accessed March 20, 2014.

[143] Stoner, pp. 72, 91-92.

[144] "Interview—Dr. Ronald Glasser: Who Really Pays the Price of War?" *Vietnam*, October, 2011, p. 16.

[145] Joel S. Franks, "Good Soldier Outlier: Dregs in the Military," *Far Outliers* (faroutliers.blogspot.com), posted October 4, 2004.

[146] Jack Todd, *Desertion: In the Time of Vietnam* (Boston: Houghton Mifflin, 2001), pp. 87-89.

[147] A former Army officer, who identified himself as FJB, on the *Wild Bill Guarnere Community Forum* (forums.wildbillguarnere.com), accessed October 13, 2014.

[148] A veteran, who identified himself as "tagandbag," on *Veterans Forum*, hadit.com, posted August 7, 2009, accessed March 13, 2014.

[149] James Ferguson is the pseudonym of a Vietnam veteran who related the story in an online bulletin board for veterans, which was accessed September 14, 2014. When I sent him an e-mail inquiring about what happened to Judd, he was surprised to learn that his post was available to anyone who surfed the Internet. Wanting privacy for all men involved, he removed the post and requested that I use a pseudonym for himself and Judd, and that I refrain from divulging the name of his unit. Of course I honored his request.

[150] LTC (Ret) John E. Gross, *Our Time* (Bloomington, IN: iUniverse, 2014), pp. 99-100.

[151] Robert S. McNamara, *The Essence of Security* (New York: Harper & Row, 1968), p. 131.

[152] Ward Just, *Military Men* (New York: Avon Books, 1970), p. 69.

153 Linda S. Gottfredson, "The General Intelligence Factor," a chapter in *Scientific American Reader for Psychology: A Concise Introduction*, edited by Richard A. Griggs (New York: Worth Publishers, 2007), p. 40.

154 Attorney David Addlestone, director of the National Veterans Law Center, telephone interview, November 12, 1979.

155 Christian G. Appy, *Patriots: The Vietnam War Remembered from All Sides* (New York: Penguin, 2003), p. 165.

156 "Army Takes Another Look at Mentally Retarded GI," *The Evening Independent*, Jan. 3, 1969, p. 9; Telephone interviews with staff members in the office of U.S. Senator Mark Hatfield, March 7-12, 1974.

157 All of the information about PFC White comes from Douglas Bey, *Wizard 6: A Combat Psychiatrist in Vietnam* (College Station: Texas A&M University Press, 2006), pp. 144-146.

158 Bey, pp. 144, 146-155.

159 Bey, pp. 141-142.

160 Raymond R. Crowe and Edward M. Colbach, "A Psychiatric Experience with Project 100,000," *Military Medicine*, March 1971, pp. 271-273.

161 Albert J. Glass, Kenneth L. Artiss, James J. Gibbs, and Vincent C. Sweeney, "The Current Status of Army Psychiatry," *American Journal of Psychiatry*, February 1961, pp. 673-683.

162 Edward M. Colbach, M.D., "Ethical Issues in Combat Psychiatry," *Military Medicine*, May 1985, pp. 259-260.

163 Rick Springman, a former prisoner of war, quoted by Joe Eszterhas, "The POW Who Laid Down His Gun," *Rolling Stone*, March 28, 1974, cover story of magazine.

164 Colonel Jack Crouchet, *Vietnam Stories: A Judge's Memoir* (Niwot, CO: University Press of Colorado, 1997), pp. 28-33.

165 Quoted by Crouchet, p. 66.

166 All of the information on "Mike Sanchez" comes from Jim Bracewell, "Sanchez," LRRP Rangers of the Vietnam War, lrrprangers.com, accessed January 17, 2014.

167 Watson, p. 154.

168 Raven Wenner, "Low IQ Didn't Limit Classmate," *Houston Chronicle*, June 12, 1994, Lifestyle section, p. 1.

[169] All the information on Harris came from a veteran who operated the blog, "Grumpy Opinions," grumpyelder.com, accessed October 3, 2014.

[170] Mark Frutkin, *Erratic North: A Vietnam Draft Resister's Life in the Canadian Bush* (Toronto: Dundurn Press, 2008), p. 84.

[171] Adam Bernstein, "Gen. Louis Wilson Dies; Awarded Medal of Honor," *Washington Post*, June 24, 2005, p. B.05.

[172] "Military Records," National Archives, archives.gov, accessed January 17, 2014.

[173] Kevin Hillstrom and Laurie Collier Hillstrom, *The Vietnam Experience* (Westport, CT: Greenwood Press, 1998), p. 135.

[174] Baskir & Strauss, p 129.

[175] Case Number 84, *Presidential Clemency Board: Report to the President* (Washington DC: Government Printing Office, 1975), p. 302.

[176] Adrian R. Lewis, *The American Culture of War: The History of U.S. Military Force from World War II to Operation Iraqi Freedom*, 2nd edition (New York: Routledge, 2012), p. 276.

[177] James Tracy, editor, *The Military Draft Handbook* (San Francisco: Manic D Press, 2006), p. 34; Sherry Gershon Gottlieb, *Hell No, We Won't Go! Resisting the Draft During the Vietnam War* (New York: Viking, 1991), p. 256; Andrew C. Carr, M.D., *The 8th Field Hospital* (Victoria, British Columbia: Trafford Publishing, 2005), p. 10.

[178] "Project 100,000 … Army for Dummies," an article posted on blogster.com by an Army veteran who used the online name, bigfatdaddy, posted on October 25, 2013, accessed February 21, 2014.

[179] Gloria Emerson, "The Good Soldier Yossarian," *Los Angeles Times*, online archives, articles.latimes.com, posted April 23, 2000, accessed March 3, 2014.

[180] Major James G. Miles, U.S. Army (Retired), *Pay Any Price* (Yigo, Guam: James G. Miles, Publisher, 1988), p. 121.

[181] James Lafferty, as quoted by Christian G. Appy, *Patriots: The Vietnam War Remembered from All Sides* (New York: Penguin, 2003), p. 165.

182 "Doctor Helps Men Avoid Military Duty," *Arizona Republic*, December 4, 1970, p. 70.

183 Bill Adams, Staff Sergeant, U.S. Army, Fort Bliss, Texas, personal interview, September 14, 1972.

184 Congressman Parren J. Mitchell, "Report from Washington: Medical Reevaluation and Review System," *Baltimore Afro-American*, July 3, 1971, p. 3.

185 David Caruso, "Called to Serve," calledtoservevietnam.com, accessed November 21, 2014.

186 Ward, p. 15.

187 Ward, p. 16.

188 Patrick Murfin, "Uncle Sam's Guest—Induction Center," The Third City (www.thethirdcity.org), posted February 1, 2012. Accessed October 13, 2014.

189 Franks.

190 Appy, *Working-Class War*, pp. 78-80.

191 Buford, p. 44.

192 "Tom DeLay," WikiQuote, en.wikiquote.org, accessed November 28, 2013.

193 Buford, p. 21.

194 Peter Tauber, *The Sunshine Soldiers* (New York: Simon and Schuster, 1971), pp. 28-29.

195 John Ketwig, *...And a Hard Rain Fell* (Naperville, IL: SourceBooks, 2008), p. 28.

196 Todd, p. 35.

197 Westheider, p. 53.

198 Dr. William.

199 Westheider, pp. 46 - 47.

200 Murray Polner, "Vietnam War Stories," a chapter in *America and the Asian Revolutions*, Robert Jay Lifton, editor (New Brunswick, NJ: Transaction Books, 1970), pp. 55-56.

201 Charles Wilson, in *Hearings on Marine Corps' Recruit Training and Recruiting Programs*, p. 4.

202 William C. Westmoreland, *A Soldier Reports* (New York: Doubleday, 1976), p. 372.

203 Westheider, p. 47.

204 Westheider, p. 47.

205 Westheider, p. 47.

206 Bey, p. 160.

207 Michael Volkin, quoted by Colonel Jack Jacobs and David Fisher, *Basic: Surviving Boot Camp and Basic Training* (New York: St. Martin's Press, 2012), p. 33.

208 Juan Ramirez, *A Patriot After All: The Story of a Chicano Vietnam Vet* (Albuquerque: University of New Mexico Press, 1999), pp. 154-157.

209 Nolan, p. 168.

210 P. J. Rice, former U.S. Army attorney, "Soldiers with Prior Criminal Records," RiceQuips blog, ricequips.com, accessed November 5, 2014.

211 Heinl, pp. 30-37.

212 Baskir & Strauss, p. 143; Gabriel, p. 12.

213 Richard Moser, *The New Winter Soldiers* (New Brunswick, NJ: Rutgers University Press, 1996), p. 48.

214 Westheider, pp. 187-189.

215 Jack Shulimson, Lieutenant Colonel Leonard A. Blasiol, Captain David A. Dawson, and others, *U.S. Marines in Vietnam: The Defining Year—1968* (Washington, DC: History and Museums Division, U.S. Marine Corps, 1997), p. 566.

216 Peter Brush, "Fragging: Why U.S. Soldiers Assaulted Their Officers in Vietnam," *Vietnam*, April, 2011, pp. 61-62 [a review of *Fragging: Why U.S. Soldiers Assaulted Their Officers in Vietnam*, by George Lepre, Texas Tech University Press, 2011].

217 Nylen, p. 70.

218 Barnes, p. 105.

219 Barnes, pp. 109-111.

220 Barnes, pp. 109-111.

221 Malcolm Miller-Jones, who served in the Armed Forces in 1967 - 1969, including service as a member of the U.S. Combat Support Element, MacDill Air Force Base, personal interview, October 7, 2014.

222 Kyle Benson, former NCO in Vietnam, personal interview at Charles George VA Medical Center, Oteen, North Carolina, November 12, 1997,

[223] Tom Halsted, "Leave Nobody Behind," *Huffington Post*, huffingtonpost.com, posted on June 10, 2014. Halsted told the story to underscore the point that the U.S. military never leaves a trooper behind—not even a malingerer.

[224] John Christian Worsencroft, *Salvageable Manhood: Project 100,000 and the Gendered Politics of the Vietnam War*, Master of Arts thesis, History Department, University of Utah, May 2011, p. 36; Colbach, "Ethical Issues," p. 259.

[225] "Service Number (SN) and Social Security Number (SSN)," National Archives, archives.gov, accessed June 15, 2014.

[226] Article from *Stars and Stripes* newspaper, June 17, 1968, reprinted on the website of the 25th Aviation Battalion, 25thaviation.org/id285.htm, accessed August 30, 2014.

[227] Don Phelps, HMC, USN (Ret), Oxnard, California, letter to the author, August 14, 1978, in response to author's query in *VFW Magazine*, June-July, 1978.

[228] Jack Durish, "Letters of Condolence," Jack Durish, jackdurish.com, accessed January 23, 2014.

[229] Harry N. Watkins, former Sergeant, U.S. Army, interviews at Charles George VA Medical Center, Oteen, North Carolina, during the fall of 1980.

[230] Ronald J. Ellefson, letter to the author, July 9, 1978, in response to author's query in *The Retired Officer* magazine.

[231] Baskir and Strauss, p. 122.

[232] Heinl, p. 5.

[233] Barnes, p. 239.

[234] Paul R. Camacho and David Coffee, "Project 100,000," a chapter in *The Encyclopedia of the Vietnam War*, Spencer C. Tucker, editor, 2nd edition (Santa Barbara, CA: ABC-CLIO, 2011), p. 937.

[235] Appy, *Working-Class War*, p. 31.

[236] Baskir and Strauss, p. 153.

[237] Presidential Clemency Board, p. 111.

[238] The information about the Presidio Mutiny comes from Peter Barnes, *Pawns: The Plight of the Citizen-Soldier* (New York: Alfred A. Knopf, 1972), and Fred Gardner, *The Unlawful Concert* (New York: Viking Press, 1970).

[239] Robert Sherrill, *Military Justice Is to Justice as Military Music Is to Music* (New York: Harper & Row, 1969), p. 21.

[240] Barnes, pp. 223-224.

[241] Sherrill, p. 25.

[242] Gardner, pp. 48-49.

[243] Ron Bitzer, Center for Veterans' Rights, Los Angeles, letter to author, August 15, 1978; Phillip Carter, "The Vets We Reject and Ignore," *The New York Times*, November 11, 2013, p. A21.

[244] Winter, p. 591.

[245] Baskir and Strauss, pp. 122-127.

[246] Anita Wadhwani, "Finding Men His Mission Again," *The Tennessean*, November 10, 2002, p. 1B.

[247] Richard Abshire, "Veteran Wants Vietnam-era Enlisting Experience Remembered, Not Repeated," *Dallas Morning News*, November 12, 2009. Online.

[248] Worsencroft, p. 2.

[249] Charles Moskos, professor of sociology, Northwestern University, letter to the author, May 16, 1978.

[250] Captain Jim Lane, quoted by Betty Brink, "A Risky Game to Harp on Vietnam Draft," *Orlando Sentinel*, October 11, 1992, D1.

[251] Starr, p. 194.

[252] William F Abbott, "The Names on the Wall: A Closer Look," *American War Library*, americanwarlibrary.com/vietnam/vwc20.htm, accessed March 23, 2014.

[253] Blogger identifying himself as Aesop, *WeaponsMan*, weaponsman.com, posted September 21, 2013. Accessed October 25, 2014.

[254] John P. Wilson, Ph.D., Department of Psychology, Cleveland State University, letter to the author, July 11, 1978.

[255] Starr, pp. 194-195.

[256] Drea, p. 271.

[257] Benedict Carey, "Combat Stress Found to Persist Since Vietnam," *New York Times*, August 8, 2014, p. A1; Gregg Zoroya, "Vietnam Veterans Still Dogged by PTSD," *USA Today*, usatoday.com, accessed August 20, 2014.

[258] Thomas Sticht, "Project 100,000 in the Vietnam War and Afterward," a chapter in *Scraping the Barrel*, edited by Sanders Marble (New York: Fordham University Press, 2012), p. 254.

259 Joe "Ragman" Tarnovsky, "Ohio Vets Hall of Fame," *Veterans Today*, veteranstoday.com, accessed August 13, 2014.

260 John W. Geymann, "Lessons Lost," *Marine Corps Gazette*, July, 2008, pp. 6, 8.

261 Shapley, p. 387.

262 Shapley, p. 388.

263 Appy, *Working-Class War*, p. 32.

264 Anni P. Baker, *Life in the U.S. Armed Forces* (New York: Praeger, 2007), p. 19.

265 Jacob Heilbrunn, "The Hollow Man," *New Republic*, March 22, 1993, pp. 31-37.

266 Samuel F. Yette, quoted in Ward, p. 9.

267 Myra MacPherson, "McNamara's 'Moron Corps,'" *Salon,* salon. com, accessed October 5, 2014.

268 Baskir and Strauss, p. 131.

269 Kelly M. Greenhill, "Don't Dumb Down the Army," *The New York Times*, p. A23, Feb. 17, 2006.

270 Charles Wilson, p. 2.

271 James R. Jones, member, U.S. Congress, from Oklahoma's First District, telephone interview, January 16, 1979; "Army's CID Probing Tulsa Recruiting Office," *The Lawton Constitution*, June 6, 1976, p. 48.

272 Bailey, p. 120.

273 Dan Ephron, "He Should Never Have Gone to Iraq," *Newsweek*, June 30, 2008, pp. 33-34.

274 "Bad Recruiting Caught on Tape," ABC News video report on *Good Morning America*, Nov. 3, 2006.

275 Dane Schiller, "Houston Marine Recruiters Busted in Exam Fraud," *Houston Chronicle* online (chron.com), posted Nov. 1, 2007.

276 Lizette Alvarez, "Army Giving More Waivers in Recruiting," *The New York Times*, February 14, 2007, p. A1; Editorial, "Moral Waivers and the Military," *The New York Times*, February 20, 2007, p. A18.

277 Jim Dwyer and Robert F. Worth, "Accused G.I. Was Troubled Long Before Iraq," *The New York Times*, July 14, 2006, p. A1.

278 David Zucchino, "Soldier Convicted in Rape, Murder of Iraqi Girl is Found Hanged," *Los Angeles Times*, February 18, 2014, p. A6.

279 Paul von Zielbauer, "Army, Intent on Sending a Message, Cracks Down on Deserters," *New York Times*, April 9, 2007, p. A10.

280 Tony Perry, "Case of Autistic Marine Brings Recruiting Problems to the Forefront," *Los Angeles Times* online, articles.latimes.com, posted July 6, 2009, accessed January 15, 2014.

281 Michael Broihier, "Robert Strange McNamara, RIP," *Central Kentucky News*, articles.centralkynews.com, posted July 15, 2009, accessed January 15, 2014.

# Index

# About the Author

Hamilton Gregory is a former Associated Press writer and the author of a best-selling college textbook, *Public Speaking for College & Career*. A Vietnam veteran, he has been a longtime advocate for the needs of veterans with physical, emotional, and intellectual disabilities.

Made in the USA
Monee, IL
03 February 2020